MY MOTHER
MY HERO

MY MOTHER MY HERO

Achyuta Samanta

RUPA

Published by
Rupa Publications India Pvt. Ltd 2021
7/16, Ansari Road, Daryaganj
New Delhi 110002

Sales Centres:
Allahabad Bengaluru Chennai
Hyderabad Jaipur Kathmandu
Kolkata Mumbai

ISBN: 978-93-5333-876-3

First impression 2021

10 9 8 7 6 5 4 2 3 1

Printed at Thomson Press India Ltd, Faridabad

Dedicated to the wondrous,
divine race of humanity—mothers.

CONTENTS

PREFACE

To Ma...
The earliest memories I have of you is when I was all of four. And today, as I look back, I'm happy and proud and grateful that you were more than a mother to me. You were a friend, a philosopher and a guide. You shaped my life and made me the person I am today. Thank you, Ma...

Our mother, Nilimarani Samanta, passed away on 2 August 2016. She was 89. She had a charismatic personality and that became all the more obvious when an overwhelming amount of messages and homages started pouring in from across Odisha and beyond, on her sad demise.

She was a mother figure to the people of her village, Kalarabanka, where she was born and raised. She was also married into a family from the same village. She came from an affluent family but was given away in marriage to a man with very little fortune. She was very pampered as a child. Her father wanted her to marry a decent man, who would love her and keep her happy, not essentially a person with wealth.

Her greatness was not only on account of her longevity or her affluent childhood. I firmly believe that it is not how long you live, but rather *how* you live that matters. Mother had used every minute of her sojourn on earth wisely and had bravely fought blows after blows that fate had smacked on her face time and again. Her journey was one of patience, indomitability and incessant perseverance—qualities which were needed in good measure to single-handedly bring up seven fatherless children. Except for her childhood, she had to struggle for a major part of her life. Most of these ordeals were what she went through to keep her children alive and to raise them. Many a time, I would find Ma weeping silently as she watched her children go to bed on an empty stomach. I had often seen tears in her sunken eyes—eyes that were once as beautiful as pearls—as they rolled down her cheeks, when she was alone, deep in thoughts.

After Father's (Shri Anadi Charan Samanta) untimely demise, the mammoth responsibility of raising seven children and running the household fell on her tender shoulders. Her struggles and hardships bore fruit when her children were well-settled in their lives and had all become people of worth in society. She always reminded us our father's words: 'Become good men and women and serve your fellow human beings in whatever endeavours you undertake.' He would go on to add: 'Whatever endeavour we undertake in life would, in fact, be an opportunity to serve mankind. Therefore, doing them diligently and deftly would mean paving the way for God's blessings to reach you.'

In hindsight, I cannot help but admire Ma's vision for the village and how much she wanted to give back to her motherland. If Kalarabanka is one of the first smart villages in the country, it is because of her vision. This transformation of the village did not happen overnight. She asked for a little financial support every time she spoke to me. It took the village five years (from 2000 to 2006) to become a model village and another ten to become a smart village. Today, the village is visited by hundreds of social workers, researchers, academicians and statesmen from across the country and the world.

Even to this day, when we visit our ancestral house, it makes us nostalgic. We had recently gone to stay there for a few days. The house, which was once like a humble cowshed, has now been extended and three more rooms have been added. If our mother wanted, she could have asked me to renovate the house and upgrade it to a double- or a triple-storied villa, or she could have asked me to buy a bigger plot of land or a bigger house. But she never did. She was content with the house she lived in and usually refurbished it on her own, as and when the need arose.

We didn't have any agricultural land in the village. We had to buy our provisions, including rice from the market, which we still do—a practice that we have not let go of, though we can now afford to buy acres of land in the village.

Our mother always wore simple, inexpensive white cotton sarees. She didn't like to have more than two sarees in her wardrobe. Even we used to get only a pair of ordinary dresses once a year. We wore them till they were worn out. Despite my mother's simple living and disposition, there were two major areas where she particularly shone: as a mother and as a social worker. No darkness could extinguish her innate flame. God had bestowed on her a tremendous life force and courage, which she exuded till she breathed her last.

When I was able to stand on my own feet, I started seeing my mother more as an individual, and not just as someone's wife or mother. I could relate to her hopes and dreams, and she became a friend, a philosopher and a guide to me. She was my hero, too. In fact, she was a hero to the entire village. To the residents of Kalarabanka, she was a mother figure and they fondly addressed her as 'Ma'. Today, people remember her struggles and her strengths, and find in her life story, the inspiration to lead a worthy life and give back to society. 'What you give comes back to you multiplied many times,' she would often say.

It was her charismatic personality, her drive and zeal, that organized the villagers to work together as a team for the development of the village. Kalarabanka has become a beacon of hope for the neighbouring villages. Today, the village has attained the status of a smart village and stands as an example for the entire country to emulate, for which all credit essentially goes to my mother. The 'smart village' tag has triggered a social revolution for the development and reconstruction of other villages as well.

My mother did not graduate from the halls of some renowned university. She did not even have the opportunity to visit a formal school, let alone study there. However, she was blessed with worldly wisdom, which she acquired from the tradition and culture that she was born into. She was like an encyclopedia of idioms, verses and short stories which were replete with life lessons. She would have a verse, an idiom or a short story ready to quote when things were going downhill.

She was a philosopher and a pragmatist. She was a captain par excellence, someone who knew how to navigate through the complexities of contemporary social system. If she had wanted, she could have lived an ostentatious life after her children were well-settled. But, she never changed. She lived in the same village house, refurbished it entirely on her own without modifying the structure, with savings from whatever money her sons sent her. If ever she had a little surplus, she would spend it on the people she knew were starving.

When her children were well-settled in life, she often coaxed them to come to the village and help her in improving the condition of the village and its residents. She did so for a higher purpose: to make her village a better place to live in and to upgrade the lives of her fellow villagers—physically, mentally and financially—so that the future generations could benefit from it.

My mother demonstrated strength of character, integrity, loyalty and commitment, even in the face of the lofty principles that she lived by and also encouraged others to lead an honourable life. Some critics said she was popular and respected because she was the mother of a popular and successful philanthropist, but I must confess, her popularity was because of her simplicity, her honesty and compassion for the poor and the hungry and her ability to endear all who crossed her path. She never demanded respect and honour. She had no desire for material wealth and personal comfort. All the respect she received, she earned on her own merit. She received admiration from people even after her death.

She did not just provide food to us; she nourished our souls too. She gave her heart and soul to grooming us. She managed the house and provided a roof over our head, she gave us a loving home. She did not just instruct us on what to do or when to do it, she actually took out the time to teach and shape us and to let us drink from her deep reservoir of wisdom and experience. Her encouragement had set me on my path. Whenever times got tough, she held up a lamp so that we could see our way forward through the pervading darkness.

It would have been natural for a woman who lost her husband at the age of 40 and for someone who lived amidst abject hunger and misery, raising her seven children, to wish for material comfort. But when her children offered her that, she gracefully declined and continued living the way she used to.

She supported me in my career of social entrepreneurship—something not every parent would do—especially when she was aware of how challenging a career choice that is. 'You have inherited your father's heart and humility, and that has always reflected in your nature,' she would often tell me. Without her guidance and tutelage, I would not have been able to accomplish what I have in life.

Like any parent, she, too, had once spoken to me about marriage and advised me to have a family of my own. But when I convinced her that that might distract me from my life's mission, she never brought it up again.

A few months after my mother's demise, one evening, as I sat reclined in my armchair after a hard day's work, I found my eyelids growing heavy and my mind drifting towards my mother and the other world. That is when the idea of writing a biography on her germinated. Through this book, I want to celebrate the lives of all mothers and their contribution to the family in particular and society in general.

Her advice was sacrosanct and I was always duty-bound to follow it. Mother was the one who taught me about the realities of life and imparted the wisdom of hard work and that I should always hold my chin up during trying times. She believed that if we don't inflict pain or suffering on others, no harm can befall us. There are many such nuggets of wisdom that she imparted on us.

Our mother took her responsibility of raising her kids very seriously. She would often say, 'Do whatever you have to, with gay abundance and feel the actual pulse of the moment.' She taught her children to be loving and duty-bound at every stage in life. And this was mostly through her actions. She led by example. I have realized those qualities as the ultimate truth and the driving force of all plausible social endeavours. She showed us through her actions that being a loving and duty-bound person entails many a sacrifice, but we should embrace it with a smile.

She was a brave soul and always wore a smile, no matter what. Even when we were struggling to manage a square meal a day, she would amuse us with humorous stories and anecdotes, and for that brief period of unadulterated laughter, life seemed easier to bear. Her laughter was robust and infectious.

On the day of her funeral and again on the tenth day after her demise, our ancestral village house received thousands of guests. She had touched many hearts with her gentle and simple acts of affection and concern. And in return, she was blessed with much love and affection even after she had left for her heavenly abode.

Time flies... The present becomes a thing of the past—intangible and almost unreal, but memories linger on—the memories of my mother's tenaciousness and grit in bringing us up, despite poverty and social alienation. The memories of the moments spent with her keep ruminating in my mind. And as I introspect, I realize that I owe everything I am and have, to her indomitable spirit and the innumerable sacrifices she had made for us.

I always feel her presence around me. Her spirit is always by my side. Her voice continues to ring in my ears, encouraging and pacifying me, and lighting the darkness that comes my way. I remember her gentle touch and how comforting and reassuring it was. I remember how she guided me when I found myself at a crossroads. The fragrance of her skin lingers on in my memory—the endearing and familiar scent when she embraced me.

Even after many years to come, our lives will never be bereft of her selfless love, of her guidance. She continues to live through us.

Her saga will continue to propel future generations. Her contribution towards her village and fellow villagers will always be remembered.

The pain of bidding her goodbye will forever haunt me.

I hope this biography inspires many a woman around the world.

I would like to express my sincere thanks to Prof. Shrikant Rath and Dr Nikita Ahya for all their support and efforts to make the content of this book very riveting. My heartfelt thanks is also due to my younger sister, Iti, for providing valuable inputs from the time this book was conceived to having it published.

1

THE JASMINE OF KALARABANKA

Though my mother's name was Nilimarani, my grandparents called her Sefali and so did her neighbours. As a child, she was brilliant, beautiful and sweet in temperament. Born into wealth and privilege, she had it all.

Sefali was born to Purnananda Samanta in 1927. Theirs was a well-to-do family in Kalarabanka, a remote but picturesque village nestled amidst sprawling greenery, extensive stretches of forests, coconut plantations, mango orchards, bamboo thickets and fertile rain-fed agricultural lands on the banks of Paika River, a tributary in the Mahanadi deltaic region in Odisha (then a part of the Bihar-Odisha province of British India). Kalarabanka was a small, quaint village; its origin dating back to the seventeenth century. It was blessed with a blissful charm and innocent heart, untouched by modernity.

During monsoons, the village would be covered in a blanket of greenery—paddy fields stretching to the horizon. During autumn, the greenery would turn into a gorgeous golden hue as the crops got laden with grains, ushering in a time of abundance, festivities and much merry-making. By the time winter would set in, the fields would turn grey after the harvest. Heaps of harvested crops could be seen lying on the fields as the mild, and sometimes harsh, northerly winds blew across the village. Following winter, pleasant and breezy summer days would set in, but soon temperatures would soar, painting the landscape a silvery glaze and making the nights sultry.

The sea of silence would be broken at daybreak by the melodious chirping of the house birds, sparrows and cuckoos. The villagers usually went about their work as the streak of golden light appeared on the eastern horizon. They would rest only briefly after lunch and then resume work in the fields, while the womenfolk got together in the courtyards, chatting endlessly. With dusk, the village folk would call it a day and head back home, content and happy. After an early dinner, they would retire for the day. Life at its simplest best!

Back in the early twentieth century, when my mother was born, accessing the village was no less gruelling than climbing Mount Everest. Cuttack was the nearest town, some 20-plus miles away. One aspiring to reach the village from Cuttack needed to travel east for about 20 miles on a bullock cart or trek along a fair-weather, narrow metal road which was laid by the British for their own administrative convenience. This road linked their headquarters at Cuttack to the traditional port of Paradip. A little before the 20th milestone on the road, one had to take a leftward diversion and continue on a cart track which tore through cropless paddy fields. Only a couple of miles of this track could be used during dry spring and summer, after which the road was intercepted by the river Paika. There was no bridge across the river.

When the river was not too shallow, a boat ferried travellers across it. When the water level receded, the villagers waded through the river to reach the other bank. Some even took their bullock carts across the shallow waters. During summer, the villagers had to plod on the wide stretch of dry sandy riverbed, which was a challenge, as the sand would get very hot. On reaching the river bank, one had to climb up the steep river embankment which was carved with vertical crooked grooves. A forest came in the way, making the travel risky, as sometimes wild animals prowled there.

Rainy days made travel all the more arduous. Paika usually overflowed during the monsoons and inundated all adjacent lands and the woodlands. This made the village inaccessible during the rains.

The village, which was primarily agrarian, was inhabited by about 600 people at that time. They lived in homesteads built by their ancestors, who had migrated from the northern regions of Odisha, several centuries ago. The villagers stayed in Kalarabanka during the monsoons and worked in the paddy fields there. The village would be bustling with activities as people went about cultivating their fields, nurturing their crops, gathering wood from the forests and tending to trees in their orchards. During the dry months, the villagers worked as migrant labourers to earn a living.

A handful of the villagers owned nearly 80 per cent of the farm landholdings comprising paddy fields, coconut plantations, mango groves, bamboo thickets and wastelands that ran into several hundred acres. The rest owned small and medium farm holdings. Actually, a large number of villagers were landless farmers or menial workers, some of whom, besides working in the fields, also worked on their landlords' homesteads. Some of them were in the business of making dairy products. They collected the surplus milk from their landlords' stables, processed them into curd, cheese or/and ghee and traded them in far-off markets. Life in the village was really tough. The farm produce did not attract fair prices. The reward from all the hard work did not tilt in favour of the labourers, which was very unfortunate. The villagers struggled, but took it in their stride. They steeled themselves to overcome every obstacle. Despite hardships, peace and love abounded in the village. The camaraderie amongst the villages was laudable and the villagers lived as one big family.

The prevailing socio-economic condition of our village and the opulence of the family my mother was born into, can be seen in her upbringing. My mother's paternal abode and the village setting indeed had a tremendous influence on her early life, and later, in the shaping of her personality during adolescence.

My grandfather had inherited a large farm landholding, several coconut plantations, mango groves, bamboo thickets and ponds, and so understandably, much opulence ensued and many generations thereafter benefitted from the inheritance. Unlike other households, my grandfather's ancestral estate didn't get divided into smaller parts with each passing generation. The homestead's appearance was suggestive of opulence and aristocracy that was becoming of the time. Several generations of their forefathers had lived on this homestead, which had cradled, sheltered, nurtured and groomed my mother's childhood too, with great love. As a child, she was happy-go-lucky, but she was polished in her manners and won over her friends with her sunny disposition.

The homestead's main gate opened towards the south. It comprised three blocks of built-up areas separated by two courtyards. The rooms were built of smoothened mud-mortar walls and thatched roofs. The south-facing block was quite spacious and although simple, it had a very functional layout, with a massive frontage, a backyard barn and a kitchen garden.

The homestead's facade stretched up to the village main road, which was only a narrow stretch. The other three sides had snake-proof fencing made of closely intertwined thin, flat bamboo strips and twigs. The village households usually reared a number of cats to scare away rodents. The fence, therefore, prevented snakes and rodents from getting into the premises.

A bamboo gate with an overarching bamboo net, which was covered with the thick foliage and red-and-white blossoms of a Madhumalati creeper, welcomed visitors. Beyond the front porch, a vestibule led one to the first open gravel and lime mortar courtyard, outlined by a raised three-foot-wide thatch-roof walkway on all sides. This walkway helped the inmates to access the other parts of the house without getting drenched during the rains.

A well-maintained garden took up most of the front lawn. The big garden was punctuated by a luxurious vegetation of tall coconut palm and areca palm trees along the fence. The garden had an assortment of flowering plants: white pinwheel, hibiscus, champa, jasmine and night-flowering jasmine (shiuli) as well as other small flower-bearing seasonal shrubs and bushes. In all its glory, the garden was a beautiful sight to behold and much talked about in the village. This garden was my mother's favourite place in the house and she loved spending time there. A swing in the centre of the garden was her favourite spot and she had fond memories of having played there with her friends.

The first block of the house comprised two large rooms, one on each side of the vestibule. The rooms, which were lime-washed, boasted of two big solid wooded windows on the south- and north-facing walls. The meticulous alignment of the windows, with beautifully carved designs, were a treat to the eyes and when left open, gave a clear view of the front garden and made the rooms airy and bright. The 20-inch thick mud-mortar walls and the bamboo-reinforced mud-mortar attic, under the thick layer of thatch roof, kept the temperature low inside the rooms during the blazing summer months. The rooms had heavy double-panelled wooden doors bearing ancient designs and motifs; the north-facing doors opened to a narrow verandah in the front of the rooms.

Grandfather usually sat on a thatch or a reed mattress in the porch during his free time. He received people lower in rank on that porch. On the eastern side of the vestibule was the living room, where important visitors and guests, usually villagers at par with his rank, were received. My grandfather spoke to them in private in this room. To the west of the vestibule was the master bedroom. My great-grandparents (i.e., my mother's grandparents) occupied this room and later it was occupied by my grandparents.

The use of furniture was not in vogue, and hence, the house didn't have any. Furniture could damage the mud floor and was not readily available, nor could the local carpenter make any. The tools required for carpentry work were not available. The house did have built-in, closed/open cupboards. The well-off households in the village used thick mattresses woven out of thrashed paddy stalks for sleeping and squatting. During daytime, however, these mattresses would be rolled up and stashed away in a corner of the room. A light mattress was used instead for squatting during the daytime. People used locally made terracotta or burnt-clay oil lamps. The use of lanterns was still not prevalent. Polanga or castor oil was used for lighting the lamps. If anybody had to venture out after dark, they would use a torch made of coconut bark and Polanga oil used as fuel. Teli families (a clan of people who specialized in expressing oil from different kinds of seeds) supplied Polanga oil to the households in exchange for paddy or other farm produce. These lamps were placed in the specially made alcoves on the walls. Unfortunately, the poor households could barely afford this locally made oil. When night fell, the entire village plunged into darkness. Moonlit nights enchanted the villagers and facilitated their movement. But people could not venture out much during the moonless nights. People returned to their respective homes before dark.

A section of the verandah, in front of the master bedroom, extended into the courtyard and in it was a potted holy basil (tulsi) plant.[1] Notwithstanding my grandmother's ignorance of religious practices, she tended to the basil plant with great care and reverence. She worshipped the holy basil plant every morning and evening after her morning and evening ablutions.

There was no temple in the village. The affluent households had a small, exclusive prayer room on the homestead, which housed the family's principal deity and sometimes, the idols of other gods and goddesses. In the south-east corner of my grandparents' courtyard, there was a small room specially constructed and dedicated for worshipping the presiding deity of the household, Goddess Dakhina Kali. The room was made of mud-mortar walls and a thatch-roof cover. A small window allowed ventilation. There were idols of Lord Ganesha, Goddess Parvati, Lord Shiva, Lord Jagannath, Lord Srikrishna, Goddess Radha and Goddess Mahalakhsmi, too. The small idols would be seated on a raised, wide wooden platform which was covered with an ornate cloth bearing applique work.

Some of the priests and their families lived in the village itself and the priest would often pay visits to those households which had their

---

[1]Tulsi is sacred for Hindus. It is considered to be the incarnation of Sati Tulsi, and therefore, is treated with much reverence, akin to that offered to a goddess. A Tulsi plant is a common sight in all Hindu households in coastal Odisha. Sati is believed to be revered and blessed by even Lord Vishnu and therefore one who worshipped the Tulsi plant daily is destined to go to heaven, the abode of Lord Vishnu, after death.

own temples. The landlords had given away some of their landholdings to the priests for providing such special service to them.

The deities were offered daily ablutions in the morning and bhog (food) was offered four times a day. The food that was cooked in the afternoon for the household was offered to the deities as well. Food would first be offered to the deities before serving it to the family members. For this reason, the kitchen was considered to be the holiest place in the homestead and was always neatly maintained, and food was cooked with utmost care and devotion. The priest usually performed the puja, including offering the food to the deities. In his absence, it was the responsibility of the male or female head of the household to perform the puja. Sometimes, a young male member of the resident priest's family came to help the family perform the ablutions and the food offerings. Grandfather, being a pious man, worshipped the deities regularly. My mother would often accompany her father to the prayer room.

The middle and the last block of the homestead had much relevance in the growing-up years of my mother. She, like the other women of the household, spent a lot of time there. The middle block comprised a row of three rooms with an underground cellar. The middle room, facing the narrow entrance hallway in the first block across the courtyard, had a wooden floor with a small opening that led to a cellar used for the safe storage of grains. The capacity of the cellar was enough to store a year's provision of grains. The entrance to the cellar was covered by a wooden slab and could be locked. The rooms over the cellar were also used for storing other household provisions. These rooms had attics, where small household tools and equipment, brass metal cooking ware and crockeries were kept. The room to the left was used as a bedroom and sometimes also as a labour room and post-natal nursing room. My grandparents occupied the room to the east of the cellar before they moved to the master bedroom in the first block after my great-grandparents passed away. Just across the storeroom on the west was a vestibule linking the first courtyard with the second open courtyard.

The second courtyard had a deep impact on my mother's knowledge of, and skill, in various household chores. At the far end of the second courtyard was the third block of rooms—a large kitchen, a spacious dining room and a wide vestibule that led to a sprawling backyard. On the north-eastern side of this courtyard, lay two heavy and circular solid stone blocks of similar size, one lying above the other with a pointed peg going through the centre of the two wheels. These wheels were the traditional food processors used for wet and dry grinding of rice, black gram and other cereals as well as for dry grinding of spices and condiments. To the south-east corner, lay a fairly large square-shaped raised platform made of stone blocks, for washing utensils, crockeries and other metal ware. These fixtures did speak of the elaborate, rich and refined culinary rituals in the household.

The vestibule of the third block had an attic where fuelwood for the kitchen was stored. Close to the wall, on the east side of the vestibule, lay the dhenki, a specially designed pounding log, made of very hard and heavy wood, for milling rice and other grains. Quite common in rural Odisha, the dhenki is also used for powdering rice to make various delicious sweat-meats, particularly pitha (traditional pancakes). The dhenki was usually operated by the women of the household or by hired female menials. The dhenki has a fulcrum supporting a weight at one end and a flat surface at the other end. The front end of the device has a protruding stud fastened to the main bar, for pounding. This end rocks up and down into an iron cylindrical receiver embedded in the ground. When someone standing at the other end exerts and releases the dhenki with force in quick succession, the pounding end goes up and down, thus pounding the grains fed manually into metal cylinder. Due to the force of the weight upon the rice in the pods, the rice and the golden-brown husk separated with ease. Great skill and practise are needed to turn the grain in the metal cylinder, into which the pounding hammer moved in and out.

The first block of the house and the first courtyard were reserved for the male members of the household, who usually conducted their business there. This courtyard was also used by the children as a play room. The second courtyard was usually buzzing with activities as the womenfolk went about doing various household chores. They would be busy throughout the day and the evening, but rested for a while in the afternoon, often indulging in gossip sessions. Grandmother had the responsibility of monitoring and supervising the domestic chores. As a kid, my mother would cling to her mother's side all day. She would also watch all the activities happening in the second courtyard with rapt attention.

The sprawling backyard had a barn to store farm equipment, grains and fodder for the animals. There was also a shed for four cows and two pairs of bullocks. The meticulously maintained vegetable garden made sure the kitchen had a fresh stock of seasonal vegetables such as eggplant, yam, plant tuber, taro root, drumstick, pumpkin, cucumber and green leafy vegetables. The backyard also boasted several mango, litchi, sapota, neem, jackfruit, bamboo and deodar trees.

When my grandfather began working at Cuttack, he added a makeshift bathroom and a lavatory at the other end of the backyard. There was a narrow cart-track towards the far end of the northern fence for the movement of cattle and bullock carts. The womenfolk were not permitted to use the main road, so they used this dirt track instead.

The womenfolk always had a number of chores lined up for the day and were thus up by daybreak. They would religiously offer their prayers to the tulsi after performing their daily ablutions. Then they would kindle the fire in the earthen stove to get on with the cooking. All this was done before the male members of the house were up. The kitchen and the dining place were out of bounds for the servants or strangers; they required cleaning and upkeep by the womenfolk of the household. All the household chores were looked after by my great-grandmother till my grandfather married and his spouse was mature enough to handle the chores independently.

Work on the homestead was usually elaborate and involved rigorous physical labour. Preparing even a simple meal was time-consuming.

The stoves in the kitchen made use of dry twigs and kerosene for kindling the fire and dry wood as fuel. Cooking or overseeing the cooking was the quintessential responsibility of the mistress of the house. She had to keep an eye on the stove as long as it was active. Any time the fire slackened, she had to adjust the flue or add more fuel. The ash and cinders from the stove had to be removed at least twice a day, a task that required her to gather them in a tray and then dump them outside in the backyard.

She had to supervise the servants who looked after the cleaning and feeding of livestock. The cows had to be milked twice a day and the cowshed, too, needed cleaning twice a day. The walls and floor of the house were smeared with a thin mud and cow dung mortar and then motifs painted on them, a ritual that was carried out once in a week. She spent almost eighteen hours attending to household chores. Fortunately, my grandparents could afford domestic help. The cooking was, however, the exclusive domain of my grandmother.

Betel nut is a common mouth freshener found in most households of Odisha. Offering paan to visitors was an important part of hospitality. One of the women servants would prepare, first thing in the morning, a pile of paan-folds for her co-workers, while a female family member prepared paan-folds for the male members and visitors. The women would deftly smear lime and catechu on the betel leaves, sprinkle some crushed supari (dry betel nut) and home-made spices, fold the leaves and secure the fold with a clove. These paan-folds would then be wrapped in a wet cloth to keep them fresh for long hours and placed in a brass container. My mother, too, learnt the art of making paan-folds and the spices used in them, although she herself abstained from having paan.

The children in the family had no say in their marriage. The decision rested with the parents and the senior-most members of the family. Grandfather was married at the age of twenty-one to someone almost seven years younger. They were a 'made-for-each-other' couple in the truest sense of the term. Undoubtedly, in those days, men and women from affluent households assigned great value to external beauty, as it was believed that one's looks was a reflection of their internal beauty. In the case of my great-grandmother this was true, as she was beautiful inside and out.

My maternal grandparents were blessed with five children—four daughters and a son. Their fourth child, a daughter, died soon after birth. My mother was the eldest, and my uncle (Mama) was the youngest, born many years later. By the time my uncle was born, my mother had already been married.

My mother was unmatched in beauty and character. She was often complimented on her beauty by relatives and neighbours, which made her sisters jealous. My mother's actual date of birth had always been shrouded in mystery. That was a time when a girl-child was not very welcome. Their birthdays were not celebrated, nor were their horoscopes prepared. We asked her about her exact date of birth many a time, but she would always evade the topic.

My great-grandmother was overjoyed when she learnt that my grandmother was expecting. Grandmother, although happy, was already fretting about how her husband and in-laws would react if her firstborn was a girl-child. Moreover, childbirth was risky then and mortality rate was high for the newborn as well as the mother due to the lack of adequate healthcare.

Experienced midwives were usually consulted for the smooth management of pregnancy and also delivery. There was no way to tell the gender of the foetus, but these midwives had some strange and secret skill, some inexplicable rationale, which helped them predict the gender of the baby. Of course, such predictions didn't always come true.

When a woman conceived for the first time, it was considered very special as she would help the family grow. A woman who conceived became an example and inspiration for other married women. The occasion was celebrated at home. A baby shower was usually thrown four to six weeks before the due date—the time was right as the pregnancy would have stabilized by then. At the baby shower, the mother-to-be received blessings and gifts.

When my grandmother went into labour, the midwife had to be immediately summoned. Grandmother and the midwife were locked inside the labour room. After a prolonged labour, the baby was born. As my grandmother lay with her eyes closed, thoroughly exhausted, the midwife held the newborn upside down and patted it on the back. The baby began to cry. When the baby's first cry fell on its mother's ears, she jerked her eyes open and looked in the direction of the cry, tears rolling down her eyes. The midwife laid the baby in a bassinet. 'It's a girl, a hearty piece of pie! She seems to have taken after you; she has dark hair and beautiful features. You are so blessed!' said the midwife, looking towards my grandmother. Then the midwife walked towards the door and announced from behind the closed door, 'The lady has given birth to a beautiful and perfect baby girl. Both the mother and the baby are safe. Congratulations!' On hearing the announcement, a wave of happiness swept over the family and the neighbours, who had come there in support.

The news of the birth of a baby girl slightly pissed my great-grandmother off and she felt embarrassed in front of the gathering. She feared that she would be made fun of by the elderly women in the village and the people who were jealous of their prosperity. Such thoughts did perturb her for some time, but that was only till she held the baby in her arms.

'Oh, she is such an angel!' said the midwife as she laid the baby in my great-grandmother's arms.

'What went wrong with your predictions this time? You had predicted that it would be a boy and I believed your wisdom and trusted your skills. But it is a girl. You are no good in making predictions these days and your skill is rather on the wane, I am afraid. I suppose you are getting old and should retire now, if I may suggest,' she faintly chided the midwife while lovingly receiving the baby girl in her arms.

The midwife had known from the very beginning that it was a girl, but she was careful not to offend the family and had falsely predicted that it could be a son, just to keep the ladies of the house happy.

Great-grandmother soon realized that she was being too harsh and came to terms with the truth and reversed her disposition. She reasoned with herself that babies, boy or girl, were both blessings. 'I'm so sorry, dear, for those unkind words; please take no offence,' she apologized to the midwife with a warm smile as she bent and kissed the baby on its forehead and showered her choicest blessings on the baby.

Grandfather was at that time lounging in the living room, anxious in anticipation. Great-grandmother rushed to him and announced the news to him. The news filled him with great joy and he asked, 'Oh, Mother, can I see the baby and the mother now? Can I hold the baby in my arms?'

After a while, my grandfather was allowed to go inside the labour room, but he was allowed to stay there only briefly to avoid any infection to the baby and the new mother. When he entered the room and closed the door after him, he found his wife in tears. He realized that the tears were of joy and of disappointment too. A straw bassinet filled with old sarees for cushioning had already been laid by her bedside. He went over and knelt beside the bassinet. 'It's a daughter. I'm sorry,' she said apologetically. 'How does Mother-in-law feel about it?' She couldn't stop sobbing. 'Are you disappointed?' she implored earnestly.

'Oh, no, not at all, you don't have to be so hard on yourself,' he said, cupping the baby's little head with his left hand and stroking the thin coat of hair on its head with his right hand. His eyes were fixated on the baby's face. He just couldn't take his eyes off his firstborn. At times, she seemed to look like her mother, and at others, like him. Her skin was like porcelain, her face like a full moon, the dark twinkling eyes set close to each other. The nose was slightly wide with pronounced indentation beneath the nostrils. The lips rose like the crest of a wave and the chin was tiny.

'Thank you for this splendid gift of life, dear. I'm happy beyond measure. I feel blessed. The birth of a baby girl is very auspicious and it is the best thing that has happened to us. This child is no ordinary girl; I don't know why but I have this feeling that she will one day be a great woman. Besides, you know that we treat girls as an incarnation of Goddess Lakshmi,' my grandfather said, gently putting the baby back in the cot and wiping the pearl-like tears of his wife.

After my grandfather left the room, my grandmother dragged herself with great difficulty and effort towards the edge of her thick straw mattress to reach closer to the bassinet. She felt a surge of emotions wash over her as she looked at her baby. Her exhaustion didn't deter her elation. She began imagining how the baby's arrival would change her life. What had once been an all-adults home would now come alive with the birth of this little bundle of joy. However, a sense of concern began to grip her. Will I be a good parent? she wondered. I will need to make huge adjustments, she reasoned with herself.

The baby had beautiful pink cheeks. 'Why, she looks like siuli (jasmine),' said my great-grandmother, and from that moment, everyone in the family started fondly addressing her as Sefali, another name for the siuli flower. Sefali flowers usually bloom during the autumn season, i.e. during Dussehra, and is offered to Goddess Durga. The sefali flower belonged to heaven and was brought to earth by none other than Lord Krishna himself. The flower, for its beauty and enchanting fragrance, was the Lord's fondest. My mother had a beautiful complexion—the colour one gets on mixing milk and vermillion, just like the sefali flowers. No wonder, my mother was called Sefali.

To my grandmother, who must have been in her twenties at the time of giving birth to her first child, the sight of the beautiful baby girl silently pervaded her heart with love and a myriad of emotions. As a child, my mother was very peaceful and playful. She observed people and what was happening around her with her little attentive eyes. Her innocent ways filled my grandmother's heart with immense happiness. She was already starting to feel like a proud mother, and why not, after all she had given birth to an angel, a beautiful girl-child.

It was mandatory at that time, for the mother and the baby to stay in the confinement of a room, for at least four weeks, before others were allowed to visit the household to meet the mother and the newborn. Thinking about this, my grandmother constantly ruminated about what remarks she would get to hear, and the croaking of contemptuous women in the neighbourhood, on the birth of a girl-child.

A month after the birth of my mother, an astrologer from a nearby village was summoned by my grandfather. It was a practice in the villages for parents to give their offspring a fair name. An astrologer was usually consulted for the formal naming ceremony. He would study the position of the constellation, the position of other planets, etc. at the time of the child's birth and the geographical position of the birthplace, etc. An auspicious day was then chosen for the naming ceremony, which was a time for festivity. Thus, my mother was named Nilimarani. As per tradition, my great-grandmother whispered the name into the baby's ear.

'She will grow up to be a fine young lady indeed, and she will live a full life,' the astrologer predicted. During the naming ceremony, the astrologer would narrate verses from the holy scriptures in Sanskrit. He would then translate the verses and annotate them for the benefit of the family. Sometimes, there would be unfavourable and disappointing predictions and the astrologers would tactfully handle such sensitive situations by offering a solution. This ensured that the family's feelings and sentiments were not hurt. The astrologer would make a drawing of the birth chart (kundli) on the mud floor with rock chalk.

'Well-balanced, unbiased and neutral she will be and...' the astrologer said after carefully reading my mother's birth chart. He suddenly paused, creating the right amount of suspense in his audience. Then he continued, 'However, her energetic disposition may at times bring social criticism.' On hearing this prediction, the family members exchanged quick and anxious glances. Once again, the astrologer took a pause from reading the birth chart, rolled his eyes, quickly scanned the faces of his audience and added a twist to cheer up the gathering, which had, by then, fallen silent following the last prediction. 'She may even come across someone important later in her life and attain great name and fame through the course of her life. Her life till then will be a somewhat...mmmm....roller coaster.' As the audience heaved a sigh of relief, the astrologer, too, smiled a crooked smile. He picked up his towel, which was on his bare shoulder, and wiped the slender line of catechu-stained drool dripping from the corner of his mouth.

Nilimarani's father looked anxious at that point. He had hoped that his baby would have the choicest of blessings. The astrologer's words disappointed him. Noticing the folds on my grandfather's forehead, the astrologer was quick to add, 'You are very fortunate, Mr Samanta, to have this child. There will be someone in her life who will recognize her talent and they will work together for some great cause. God has already blessed you so well, sir.' Pleased on hearing those words, my grandfather rewarded the astrologer with a hefty sum.

The second child was born three years later. By the time, the fifth child (a boy) was born, my mother was married. The youngest child, my uncle, was almost eighteen years younger to my mother.

By the time she was six, my mother had stolen everybody's hearts with her warm disposition and affectionate smile. She looked divine and such was her grace that it would freshen up even a dull day. People were all praise for her beauty. But she always stayed humble and never let the compliments get to her head. She would modestly blush though.

With time, Nilimarani grew up to be a fine girl of true faith, true to the astrologer's prediction. All she needed was to believe in something and her work would be done. Even before she turned fourteen, she had developed a knack for comprehending people rather effortlessly, a trait she inherited from her father. She communicated well. She was very friendly and could easily mingle with people of all ages. She nurtured a large heart that ached for the needy and was always ready when it came to helping them. She was witty for her age and had developed a knack for snubbing people if they tried to put her down, something that was a cause of concern for her father.

When Nilima was a few years old, my grandfather got into government service as a clerk in the postal department in Cuttack, some 20 miles away from our village, a distance that was really hard to negotiate those days. The job offer had come out of the blue. A good job, a hefty salary and respect—my grandfather couldn't say no. Later, he came to know that a distant cousin had got into the government's postal department service at Cuttack and it was he who had recommended his name for the job. The British administrators considered appointing influential and affluent Indians to work in the government posts and that's how Grandfather was referred for the job. Grandfather ascribed his good fortune to Nilima, his Goddess Lakshmi.

My grandfather began staying in Cuttack for most days in a month, thus leaving the entire responsibility of managing his estate to his wife. When he came to the village, which was once in a month, he would keep himself busy with various engagements relating to cultivation of the large landholding, which he had had inherited and those he had added on his own over time. As soon as he reached home, the children, under the leadership of my mother, would get busy ransacking his bag, looking for goodies—toys, foreign biscuits and English apparel. For the kids, the day was no less than a celebration.

He would visit his farm and issue directions to the menials working there. He had even leased some land to a few sharecroppers and needed to remain in touch with them. This way, he exercised tight control on the cultivators who worked on his lands and kept a tab on sharecroppers as to how they dealt with his land. He offered loans to the villagers and so had to chase the debtors for timely repayment of interest and principal. He would call on the difficult and belligerent debtors, and often engage in bitter haggling with them. He was known for his meticulous accounting and deft management of his farms. The young Sefali often accompanied her father on his official rounds of the village and picked up a few tricks of the trade too. His refined manners and wit in such dealings had a deep impact on her during the formative years.

The household always abounded with joy and abundance. Although the girls took delight in playing with hand-made dolls and running around the house, they did help out with the household chores, too. They ran around in the house from dawn to dusk under the watchful eyes of a couple of maidservants. Their world was an endless expanse that comprised everything within the house and the boundary of the homestead. But Grandfather's long absences from the village and the general pampering, as found in most affluent households, brought some behavioural changes in the Samanta girls, particularly in Sefali, the eldest. The opulence and freedom, which was not common in the case of the other girls, made her a bit heady and arrogant.

She would, at times, run into the garden, to the mango orchards beyond the fringe of the village, to the village forest, and sometimes in summer, to the dry riverbed of the Paika, where she would be joined by other girls, some her age, some younger and some older to her. They played kabbadi and *Bahu Chori*. During the rainy season, the girls frolicked around in the mud. They also made dolls of clay dough, splashed about in the rains and made small boats out of the banana plant's stem. The girls were never discouraged from playing for long hours for there was nothing else for them to do. Strangely, the children in the village rarely fell sick although they played in the rain and mud all day.

The kids in the village also played hide-and-seek, hopscotch (the most popular with the young girls) and Dark Room. Like busy bees, they would run amuck among the flower beds in the garden of their homesteads, carefree and happy. Sometimes, the girls would assemble in one of their friend's house and play their favourite game: doll wedding. They would divide themselves into two groups—the groom's side and the bride's side. The bride's side, headed by two of the members acting as the bride's parents, would dress up a doll in a bride's attire. The groom's side, also headed by two members acting as the groom's parents, would dress up another doll like the groom. They would use old sarees for this purpose. The traditional wedding ceremony would then be enacted. Somewhere in between playtime, there would be a mock fight between the bride's side and the groom's side over dowry and flaws in the rendering of appropriate hospitality. However, the disputes would be resolved soon and the bride would go to the groom's house. At the end of the game, the children would be treated to a sumptuous home-cooked feast in the friend's house where the play was being enacted. The game was great fun and educative for the girls, who learned how to socialize with friends and relatives.

The girls also loved to play *Andha Putuli,* an indigenous version of Blind Room. One of the girls would be blindfolded by a mutually agreed upon set of rules. The blindfolded girl would then seek out the other players, who would be hiding.

During the rainy days, the children sometimes stayed at home and played an indigenous version of Ludo. Lines were drawn on the floor and cells carved out. In place of coloured dots, different coloured stones or cowries were used.

Manufactured dolls and toys were out of reach. Some of the toys the girls played with were bought from local vendors, who visited the village during festivals. These toys were made either of clay or wood. As the girls grew up, they were encouraged to make their own toys using clay dough. They made model houses, tiny clay pots, bowls, plates, animals, dolls, birds, fruits, etc. Sometimes, the elders would make pinwheels out of coconut palm leaves and the kids enjoyed running around with those in their hands.

The river was like a friend to the children in the village. They learnt to swim very early on and my mother was no exception. They would all enjoy frolicking in the water after a long day of games and activities. A great way to unwind indeed!

My mother was an independent girl and this trait was beginning to reveal itself as she grew up. One day, she asked her mother why her birthday was never celebrated like the other boys'. Grandmother very affectionately explained to her that it was not a custom to celebrate a girl's birthday. But my mother insisted that her birthday be celebrated like the boys'. With time, she developed a strong sense of knowing what she wanted and also a streak of rebellion against the prevalent biased customs and practices.

On her sixth birthday, Mother insisted on having a celebration at home. It was not common to celebrate a girl's birthday. When she was discouraged from having a birthday party, she threw a fit. She even went on a hunger strike, so her parents had to relent. They agreed to have a 'pitha party' at home in the evening. My mother was allowed to invite her friends to join in the feast. There were about a dozen girls in the house to celebrate my mother's birthday. They played and chit-chatted all evening. My mother gladly shared the sweetmeats and pitha prepared by my grandmother with all her friends, showing unstinted generosity which was characteristic of her. She was particularly caring towards the girls younger to her. My grandmother was cautious enough to mention to the friends that it was on my mother's insistence that they had to arrange the pitha party, as she did not want any backlash from the womenfolk of the neighbourhood for crossing the line laid down for them.

Grandfather's house always received many visitors: neighbours, relatives and friends. Some guests came from far-off villages on special occasions. Young Nilimarani enjoyed being amidst friends and relatives. This exposure served her well in life, as she learnt to socialize and be hospitable. When any relative visiting the house got ready to leave, she would burst into tears and sulk. On being queried, she would insist that the guest stay with her and play.

2

THE FORBIDDEN REALM

Orissa Province was a province under British India. It was created in April 1936 due to the partition of the Bihar and Orissa Province. First, it was considered an outlying area of the Bengal Province and later, a constituent of the Bihar-Orissa Province of British India. Odisha, during those days, bore the telltale signs of British subjugation: backwardness and poverty.

In the Odia-speaking tracts, formal education at the primary level was a distant dream. Obviously, formal education was still in its nascent stage, to say the least. It was more of a dark, forbidden realm. The British rulers never wanted education to spread extensively throughout India. The British pattern of formal education was mostly restricted to a few aristocratic families of the state residing in the provincial capitals and other administrative centres, such as Cuttack. The British wanted to develop an Indian 'educated' class to help them in administration and to occupy subordinate administrative posts.

Being essentially agrarian in nature, life in Kalarabanka revolved around agriculture and horticulture. Other important activities included fishing, cattle-rearing, dairy, weaving, pottery, making of earthen tiles and weather forecasting. Learning these skills was paramount. Some even specialized in advanced skills such as Ayurveda. It was, however, very rare for people to have any formal education. The prevailing pattern of education in the villages was traditional and primitive. They had a 'chatasali' (very similar to the small grammar schools in Medieval England), where a teacher (guru) taught children how to read, write, speak and compute in the local language. These schools did not make use of books and the students were taught by rote. The students essentially depended on the skill and the ability of the teacher to help them learn and recall. Most teachers themselves were inadequately educated. The strength of the class, in some of the larger chatasalis, was ten or more boys (no girls, though they were accepted at a much later stage), and they were at school for almost ten hours, from early morning to sunset, with breaks for meals. Pupils were severely punished for mistakes made during lessons. Strict discipline was imposed on the pupils' conduct and behaviour. Caning was a common method used to bring order and discipline in the classroom.

When we think of modern education, we visualize boys and girls going to school, but this was not the case then. Only the higher classes had access to education. Women were not expected to pursue a career and therefore, were not allowed to have formal education. They were expected to help with the household chores, get married and bear children. It was difficult for a peasant's son to receive formal education and almost impossible for a girl. However, in a few well-to-do families, girls were allowed to study religious scriptures. Even if they knew how to read, they were unable to write.

The citizenry was divided into four distinct social strata (*varnas*): the Brahmins, the Kshatriyas, the Vaisyas and the Shudras. The Brahmins, who were considered nobility, wielded great power and authority, as they were believed to be the direct link to the gods and goddesses. The next in order were the Kshatriyas. It included royalty and soldiers. Then there were the Vaisyas, the class comprising businessmen and moneylenders. The Shudras were men and women who earned their living off menial labour; they were the last and the lowest class in order of respectability. The peasant community also came under this category. The Brahmins, the Kshatriyas and the Vaisyas were considered to be the upper classes and the Shudras were treated as the lower class. Because of this class division, education was not a shared privilege. The first three categories had access to education, whereas the last category did not.

It was, of course, not mandatory for the children of the upper classes to be educated. The main motive of the traditional education system was to impart moral values and scriptural literacy. At that time, there weren't many subjects offered as part of the curriculum. Also, religion had a big influence on education.

The parents were keen on introducing their children to their family businesses as early in life as possible, so that they would learn the tricks of the trade. Therefore, sending children to the chatasali was only optional. The final say rested with the parents. Only a few children, mostly from well-to-do families attended the chatasali. No time frame for completion of studies was prescribed, nor was there any prescribed age limit for enrolling in a chatasali. However, it was considered better if the pupils started their education early. The parents decided if the child was to continue with his/her studies or not. For many students, learning was a daunting task. Unable to cope, some dropped out of school shortly after enrollment. A few, however, were fast learners and they continued their study of the religious scriptures. Some even went on to specialize in more advanced mental mathematics and basic practical accounting.

One teacher taught all subjects at all levels. Sometimes, the main teacher would co-opt another teacher from his family or from the noble citizenry to assist the principal guru of the chatasali. The teachers were regarded as the most learned and wisest in the village. They commanded great respect. The teacher didn't demand any fee for their service, but it was obligatory to pay a dakshina of cereals, fruits, vegetables, milk, milk products or fuelwood. No examination was conducted to assess the students. The guru's remark was sacrosanct; if the guru said to a pupil that he had completed his learning satisfactorily, that was good enough. No certificate, of any kind, was issued as a token of the pupils' merit or level of education.

There were no blackboards, slates, paper or chalk sticks in the schools. Pupils were seldom instructed to write and if they were, they did so on the mud floor with soft rock-chalks provided by the teacher on payment of a few dimes. Some students even used charcoal. The teacher would write the lessons on the mud walls. Advanced learners would practise writing with slender pointed iron rods (*lekhani*) on palm leaves.

But there was something very interesting about the chatasali. The children learned yoga as the first lesson of the day. That was good for developing the intellectual faculties of the students. Sometimes, the guru would use specific yoga poses for punishing the undisciplined, naughty, truant and wayward students. Bad manners were not tolerated. The children also learned social manners and etiquette at school. Thus the learners were initiated to a disciplined life much early in life. Because of this, the students were refined in their manners, behaviour, conduct and speech.

As the upper-class households had some business of their own, the student would eventually become an apprentice in their family business—weaving, carpentry, agriculture, horticulture, fishing, boat-ferrying, pottery, accountancy, practising Ayurveda, and so on. By the time the children turned sixteen, they were proficient in their trade. By this time, they were considered adults and even ready for marriage.

Life in the village was simple and not many people received formal education in our village. However, Raghunathpur, a village that was about five or six miles from Kalarabanka, was then coming up as a semi-urban centre because of its strategic location. It was the road that linked the town of Cuttack to the natural port of Paradip. Unfortunately, Raghunathpur was not accessible from Kalarabanka due to obstacles such as rivers and thick forests. Hence, the villagers of Kalarabanka couldn't send their children for formal schooling there.

Purnananda Samanta, my grandfather, was born into an illustrious family in Kalarabanka and belonged to the second-most revered social class, the Kshatriyas. He was a descendant of one of the first few families that came to settle in Kalarabanka village. He was also the first and the only middle-English-school educated man of the village.

He wanted his children to have the best of everything in life, even the best of education. Unfortunately, the society at that time was orthodox and patriarchal and it opposed women's education. Parents didn't consider their daughters as valued members of their family because they were married off at a young age and sent off to live with their husband's family. A woman's job was to serve as a housewife, raise kids and perform the usual household chores.

Women didn't even have the freedom to conduct themselves. The appropriate way for a woman to conduct herself was decided by the men. The code of conduct for women was not written but handed down from one generation to the next. The women of the village had to cover their heads and faces with a veil. They could not meet or speak to men who were not their close relatives. They would rarely speak with those male relatives who were the same age as them or older. Women were not even allowed to use the main road of the village. They had to use the dirt track running along the backyard of their house. If ever they came to the main road, their faces were to be entirely covered. 'Male domination must continue,' asserted the bigots. Under such prevailing social conditions, educating the girl-child was out of the question.

However, some women, after marriage, took some time out from their daily chores to learn a thing or two from their husbands or other family members, if they were literate. Such women could read and write and even do basic calculations. Some could even read the scriptures. But this was all kept under wraps. These families would remain discreet about their women being literate.

With the passage of time, however, society began to soften its stand on the education of young girls. As no primary school was established in the village, the elite families began sending their sons to the chatasali. During the early twentieth century, the chatasali would have an exclusive session for girls.

During those days, having a girl-child was frowned upon. The birth of a girl was not celebrated as was a boy's. The boys would eventually grow up to be breadwinners and were, therefore, regarded as important members of the families and society. Once the girls were in their teens or had attained puberty, they were expected to stay at home.

With the advent of the twentieth century, young girls began questioning these restrictions and biased social norms, albeit rather meekly. They also began protesting male supremacy. Such protests were limited to the inner courtyards of the household and the voice of protest was not allowed to drift beyond the walls of the house. The subjugation of women was beginning to wane though. However, whenever such protests on discrimination spilled over, the conservative sections raised a hue and cry and tried to shush the dissenting voices. The girls' mothers would be questioned whenever such issues rose.

However, by the 1930s, the rigid views on girls' education had begun to ease substantially. Some progressive parents began sending their daughters to the local chatasali. My grandfather, who was a supporter of girl's education, began taking more tangible steps in that direction. Grandfather had initiated the opening up of a primary school. That was around the time his daughter, Sefali, was about to be born. He held discussions with a few progressive and influential people of the village. He proposed to pool the available resources needed to start a primary school. He knew that primary education was crucial for the village's growth and to keep up with the changing times. However, this proposal received a lukewarm response and he didn't pursue it further.

My grandfather stayed in Raghunathpur most of the time and although he wanted my mother to be educated, he could not take out enough time to teach her. And my grandmother was illiterate. So when Sefali was seven, her parents with the consent of her grandmother, decided to introduce her to formal education—something in contrast with the then-existing social norm.

One fine morning thereafter, my grandfather along with his daughter lumbered on to the village chatasali. The school was in session when they reached the guruji's house. They seated themselves on the bare mud floor on the front porch. When the class was over, the guruji came out to greet his guests. Nilimarani bowed and touched Guruji's feet with her forehead, while her father made the formal introductions. Guruji placed his palms on her head and blessed her, 'Long live, my child! I see you are well-groomed. What is your name, my child?'

'Nilimarani Samanta,' she replied. Guruji was pleased with her reply.

Guruji was brahmin by caste and wore his divine thread, *yagyonpabita*, over his bare shoulder. He brought with him a thin mattress which he spread out on the floor and requested my grandfather and mother to be seated. My mother, however, didn't sit down, knowing fully well that it would be tantamount to discourteousness on her part. So she moved to the farthest end of the porch and stood there instead. My mother's gesture and mannerism didn't go unnoticed.

'Guruji, will you accept Sefali as your chatra (student)? She is above six years of age—the eligible age to get admitted to the school,' my grandfather said.

Guruji turned his gaze towards Nilimarani and asked, 'Will you study?'

'Yes, Guruji!' she quickly replied, her head lowered in respect.

Guruji smiled and beckoned her to come near him. When she complied, he placed his palm on her head again and said, 'Bless you, my child. You will make a good student.'

He then summoned his junior, who was tutoring a batch in the front courtyard. Guruji introduced him to my grandfather. When both exchanged greetings, Guruji turned towards his junior and said in a solemn tone: 'Here is a pupil whom I recommend. Her name is Nilimarani. She will be in the beginner form. If her work and behaviour are satisfactory, she may be allowed to enter one of the upper forms, as you will judge suitable for her age and background.'

Nilimarani walked to the teacher, kneeled, bowed her head till it touched his feet and he blessed her, 'May God bless you, my girl. Follow me to the class.'

Nilimarani followed him like a calf following its mother. Once she was in the class, the teacher signalled her to stand by his side and addressed the class: 'She is Nilimarani Samanta, the new addition to this class.'

The class clapped in unison to welcome the new student. Once the introduction was over, the teacher asked her to sit at the end of the girls' row. As there were very few girls, there was no separate session for them. The boys and the girls were seated on the floor in two separate rows. Soon, the teacher resumed the lesson. They were being taught the letters of the alphabet. The class repeated the letters after the teacher.

The first session ended soon after and the students prepared to return to their respective homes. Nilimarani's chaperon was still there, awaiting her return. Together, they returned home.

Soon, Nilimarani learned the letters of Odia alphabet and to count. She also learned how to write sentences and do simple mathematics. The syllabus required students to read and write simple texts and some basics of grammar. The students learned short stories and short poems, too.

On any given day, my grandparents' house would be bustling with activities. Although there were servants to attend to the chores, my grandmother kept a strict and close vigil on them. She was admired for her levelheadedness, intelligence, kindness and humility. She was soft-spoken and admirably graceful. She managed the affairs of the household efficiently and to the satisfaction of her husband. The maids working in the homestead respected her, for she even lent them a helping hand at times. Sefali grew up watching her mother manage the household and this instilled a deep sense of discipline in her, too.

Nilimarani was very fond of her grandmother. When she returned home after playing with her friends and running around the house, her grandmother would pull her, place her on her lap and wipe the sweat off her face with her saree's kani (the free end of the saree). She would lovingly say, 'Oh, my sweet little angel!' and wrap her in a tight embrace and give her a quick smack on her forehead.

Every night, Nilimarani would fling herself into her grandmother's lap and she would affectionately run her fingers through the young girl's silken hair. Her grandmother was a repository of mythological stories and personal anecdotes. Like most grandmothers, she was a great storyteller and Sefali would listen to them with rapt attention and awe. Her grandmother's stories were replete with Odia and Bengali idioms, phrases, stories and verses speaking of the exaltedness of morality and were full of worldly wisdom. My mother not only memorized those idioms and phrases, she even understood their true meaning.

Her grandmother's stories were mostly about women in mythology and also about the lives of other women of her time—their accomplishments and failures, their joys and disappointments. These stories left a deep impression on my mother's mind.

By the time Sefali turned ten, there were voices of disapproval in the family about her going to school. People at home whispered, 'Why does she have to go to school? She will get married. There will be many suitors for her—sons of businessmen, landlords and rich farmers who would be eager to marry her. It is time she learnt household chores. After all, looking after the family is a girl's ultimate goal.' Her literacy journey would have come to an end had her father not intervened.

Grandfather promptly arranged to send Nilimarani to a vernacular-medium primary school at Raghunathpur. A bullock-cart took her to the river bank, from where she was ferried across to the other side of the river. There, another bullock-cart waited to carry the child to school. The cart would wait to bring her back to the riverbank. She was, of course, always accompanied by her chaperon. Thus she completed her primary schooling.

She was a bright student, far brighter than the other girls in her class and she had even beaten the boys in many subjects. While she was particularly good at the literary subjects and crafts, her interest lay in classical literature and poetry. Her wit and presence of mind amazed her teachers and she was their favourite student. She would often surprise them with her repository of idioms and verses that she learnt from her grandmother. She had indeed been an exemplary student. Her teachers would often say, 'Look at this girl, she is destined to touch the skies.'

It, however, cannot be denied that she was luckier compared to other girls of her age; even most of her cousins didn't get to attend school. The small school was like paradise to her and she was a fragrant rose in that paradise. However, her formal schooling was not to last very long.

3

A FIRST TWIST OF FATE

During those days, parents gave their daughters away in marriage as soon as they attained puberty. Marriages were, then, solemnized not for love but for convenience and to adhere to prevalent social norms. A girl was expected to get married at a tender age, bear children and raise them, and help out with the household chores. Child marriages were rampant, too. Marriages were arranged after talks between both sides of the families. Sometimes a man would end up marrying a girl half his age. Early pregnancy was a threat to the health of the mother as well as the baby. Female mortality was quite high. Cases of dowry-related atrocities on women, bride burning and torture were common, too.

The teenage girls (and some as young as ten years old) in the village would be busy learning the household chores and they would be instructed to stay indoors. Even if they were allowed to venture out, it was not beyond the premises. During this time, the young girls were groomed to look after the house, as that is what was expected of them after marriage, too.

The view of Kalarabanka's residents on a child's marriage was not very different from that of the rest of the Odia-speaking tracts, which had by now become a new province, Odisha. Here, too, most girls would be let off in marriage by fourteen years of age.

When the girls were of a marriageable age, they would be put under a lot of pressure to learn the chores. My mother, however, had it slightly easy, as there was help around the house who took care of the chores, except the cooking. It was considered a major offense to serve food to male members by menstruating women. The kitchen was out of bounds during those days for menstruating women and even the married women had to sleep in separate bedrooms. It dawned on Sefali at that time that rules were different for boys and girls and a woman can be in exile even in her own house.

Although born to luxury, my mother had an adventurous streak in her. Some of her neighbours even considered her to be a flighty little country girl and even 'wild'. She had acquired a steely stubbornness by then, perhaps because of too much pampering by her father. Nilimarani, of course, was blissfully unaware of what was coming and so was still very playful. Her play area was restricted mostly to their garden, the front porch and the first courtyard. Her friends hesitated to play games that required running around. Instead, they preferred to sit in groups and talk about their mood swings, feelings and apprehensions about their future life, as they couldn't share these openly with other members of their family.

The mothers counselled their girls not to talk back to elders, especially the male members. They were trained to wake up before sunrise and finish their daily chores of ablution and cleaning the house, including cleaning the kitchen as early as possible—sometimes even before the rest of the household was up. The mud-mortar homes required frequent upkeep and it was part of a woman's duties to smear mud mixed with cow dung on the floors and walls. If there was any slip-up in performing their designated chores, the young girls were reprimanded.

Sefali soon began to realize that her group of friends was beginning to taper off. When she saw that her most of friends were getting married, she began to experience a strange, unsettling feeling. She grew jittery and lonely; innumerable thoughts jostled in, and tormented, her otherwise calm and playful mind. Her usual countenance was affected by growing tension and she could feel the noose tightening around her neck. However, she was unaware of what was going on in her father's, or for that matter, her mother's mind. 'Ah, my parents must be out of their senses to let their loved daughter off in marriage at this tender age; certainly the cruelest thing to happen to a fourteen-year-old girl!' she thought to herself.

'A girl's true home is with her husband' was something girls were made to accept early in life. Perhaps that is true, Sefali often wondered and she shuddered at the thought. The idea of marriage made Sefali feel insignificant, like she was the teeniest drop in a wide ocean and her parents did not even take notice of the anxiety and doubts brewing inside her. The life of a woman is indeed insignificant! They often are the unsung heroes. She felt the ground slipping under her feet. All those thoughts made her pensive and the overwhelming emotions choked her.

After finishing her morning ablutions, Sefali would often sit in the verandah, lost in thoughts. She would carelessly curl her long and beautiful hair with her fingers as she sat there thinking about the future.

Sefali was very close to her father and she always sought his opinion on everything. If she got a new haircut, she would run to her father, and not her mother, in excitement. And now that she was so troubled by the thoughts of marriage and her future home, she missed her father and his guidance all the more. But her father had to go out of the village for work every day. Her journey through adolescence was mostly navigated by her mother.

As a teen and young adult, she struggled with insecurities and depression, like any other girl at that age, and she turned to her father for assurance that everything was right. Her father would leave home early for work to Raghunathpur and her mother stayed busy supervising the household chores. As the first postmaster of the newly opened post office and being a local, a great amount of responsibility rested on her father's shoulders. The post office was a new addition to the village and the villagers needed assistance. Thus, her father had to address most of the concerns and queries and he was left with very little time to think about what was happening back home.

Too tired and exhausted with thinking about marriage and what the future held, my mother decided to live in the moment. So she started to volunteer to lend a helping hand to her mother and other maids in the house and this pleased everyone in the family. She tried to get up early like the other girls in the neighbourhood.

People in the village were an orthodox and prejudiced lot. Though the social norms were very biased, they were accepted with vehement obstinacy and any violation of the customs and tradition was met with severe consequences. Women did not have the power to resist the prevailing social customs and practices. The girls couldn't take their own decisions, not even those related to their own life. They had to take the permission of the senior-most male member of the family and the community for each and every issue that meant/entailed stepping out of the convention and were in contrast to the followed rules. They didn't have any say in important household matters and certainly not in the matter of their own marriage.

In keeping with the existing norms, the senior male members of the family usually fixed the marriages. The girls were never consulted but were *told* to marry a man whom her family chose for her. The girls were counselled to abide by the whims and fancies of their husbands, without fail. Going against the husband's wishes was considered a sin. In marriage, the husband always had the upper hand. It was as if the groom was doing a favour by marrying the girl and the family expected the favour to be returned in the form of a fat dowry.

As mentioned earlier, Sefali had developed a stubborn streak owing to the love and attention she received during her growing-up years, especially from her father. Her stubbornness had become the point of discussion, or rather fodder for gossip, for the women in the village. They would often complain to her grandmother about Sefali's adventurous escapades and point out flaws in the way she was being groomed. 'You ought to know better. We were brought up differently. It's absurd and quite unbecoming of you to have spoilt Sefali like this. Now the other children also are beginning to follow in her footsteps. I wouldn't have put up with such behaviour if she were my daughter. You should not pamper them so much. You must discipline the girls and make them worthy of a good groom,' said one of the elderly women during one of the afternoon gossip sessions, almost shocking my grandmother.

'Ah, Sefali's mother, if only you took heed of our advice, it would have helped in complementing her God-gifted beauty and make her a fine bride,' said another, pulling the *kani* over her head to her mouth and biting the other end in a corner of her catechu-smeared teeth.

When Sefali talked, people thought she was being impertinent. When she chose to be quiet, people thought she was being proud and naive. If she answered back or explained something, it was considered rude. If she dared to share a new idea or thought, she was branded as sly. If she got tired, she was told it was not good to be lazy. If she ate a mouthful more than she should, she was advised not to be a glutton and be more 'ladylike'.

My grandmother always heard them out patiently but didn't really care too much about what they had to say. She would usually flash an uneven, often crooked smile at them, as she knew that they were jealous and wanted to flaunt their parenting wisdom as per traditional social norms. She knew her girls better. Sefali's mother, too, would quickly and wittily change the topic but would later gently admonish her daughter to be more careful in future.

In the village, it was considered impolite to not listen to elders. At first, Nilimarani was unhappy about being asked to stay at home but later, she agreed and started spending most of her leisure hours playing with her shy younger sisters within the premises. She wished her sisters took part in her pranks, but they were more reserved and shy.

Although my grandmother was amused by the frequent remarks made by the womenfolk about Sefali's conduct and her childlike ways, she did worry for her. One day, while informing her husband about what the women in the neighborhood thought of and said about Sefali, she pleaded, 'Hearken, Sefali's father, our daughter is growing up to be a beautiful girl and before soon, she will have to be given away in marriage. We must find a suitable match for her. You know her temperament, right?'

'Ah, those malicious women! They are so naive and crass!' Grandfather remarked with a smirk, for he knew his daughter better and their opinions didn't change how he felt for her. She was very dear to him, she being his firstborn. Grandfather knew that despite her stubbornness and carefree nature, she was soft and tender at heart. 'You have reminded me of my duty towards my daughter well in time. Thank you, Sefali's mother!' he said as he treated himself to a paan served by his wife.

In Indian society, a girl's virginity is given utmost importance when it comes to marriage. Parents who didn't get their daughters married off at the right age were stigmatized. My grandfather didn't fear being stigmatized and he was not in favour of early marriage. He was, however, aware of the piercing comments the women in the household had to hear when their daughters were not married off at the right age.

He was inwardly happy that his daughter would soon be married off and he would become a part of the fathers-in-law group of the village. However, his happiness was short-lived, as he soon realized that that would also mean giving away this daughter to someone else and that 'someone else' will take his place in his daughter's life. Her wedding was an important rite of passage. Being the father of a bride was a big responsibility for just about every father at the time. Laden with fears, emotions and with a desire to build a positive life for the daughter, finding a suitable groom in the first place could make the best of fathers everywhere to break into a cold sweat. It was wonderful to see one's daughter grow up, get married and start her own family, but the events surrounding the whole experience of separation of father and daughter was fraught with pain. Coming to the realization that his daughter would soon be part of a new life and a new family was tough. And it was even tougher as he had no idea yet what his would-be-son-in-law would be like. The thought of his daughter's marriage really overwhelmed him. But he had to go with the flow of tradition and cultural rituals.

To find a groom for his daughter, who was so beautiful and well-groomed, was for sure, a daunting task and an ultimate challenge. He quickly decided on the requisites for a deserving son-in-law and began his search. The prospective husband had to be well-bred, well-behaved, kind-hearted, forgiving and presentable to look at. Position and wealth did not matter much to him. The boy had to come from a good family and should be compatible with his daughter. He was always concerned about her safety and well-being. He had brought her up with so much love and care. All her needs were met with urgent attention.

My grandfather soon realized how challenging and daunting a task it was turning out to be. Although she was the apple of her father's eye, she was, at times, a tough nut to crack. He, therefore, wanted her to marry in the same village and into a family he knew well. He wanted his dearest daughter to be in front of his vigilant eyes. Her safety was his primary concern.

Sefali had no objection to getting married, as she knew it was a social institution and she would have to eventually marry because staying as a spinster meant living a life of shame and ridicule.

From her childhood, my mother was a believer in various cultural and religious practices and traditions. However, she had innumerable queries and she asked her parents many questions. If she was not convinced about a particular tradition or custom, or found it to be biased and unscientific, she did not hesitate to reject it. For example, fasting or not eating fish during certain religious occasions was something she did not agree to. However, she chose not to openly reject a religious or cultural practice, as she did not want to hurt anyone's sentiment.

My mother was blessed with a strong sixth sense. She could gauge the character of a person from a mile away and if she did not want to interact with someone, she would distance herself from that person without him/her knowing. When she made up her mind, she stood by her decision. Nothing could make her change her mind. She was not a conformist.

My mother had set her own benchmarks for life—simplicity, sincerity, rationality and honesty. Give her a million dollars and ask her to join the rat race, well, you have had it. However, my mother never hesitated in apologizing if she was in the wrong and her apologies came straight from her heart. But if she was made to apologize for something she hadn't done, all hell would break loose. Her face was very expressive and gave away what she felt. Faking an expression? She couldn't and never did.

Time was tip-toeing by and what was once the present was soon becoming something of the past. However, each passing day unfolded a new page of life for my mother, bringing with it new emotions and feelings and also the realization that she was at the threshold of a new life with a new person, leaving behind her own parents and family. In the meantime, my grandfather was still on the lookout for a perfect groom for my mother; it wasn't an easy task to find a perfect match for his near-perfect daughter.

When my grandfather met Anadi Samanta, the only son of Bhagaban Samanta, also from Kalarabanka, at a social function, he was thoroughly impressed. Anadi had all the qualities he was seeking in a son-in-law. To my grandfather, Anadi was Mr Right. Anadi was strikingly handsome, smart and genteel and had a cool temperament. His manners were admirable. He was a resident of the same village, Kalarabanka and belonged to the same caste as my mother's family. Anadi was very enterprising too. He supported his father in his dairy business.

It was only later that Grandfather came to know that Samanta's family was not very well-to-do. My grandfather did not respect or disrespect a person until he had ample reasons to do so. He would look through the depths of peoples' eyes and instantly figure out whether that person was a scoundrel or a gentleman at the core. He didn't go by what others said. If a person had strength of character and was ethical, he would be the recipient of my grandfather's unconditional respect and admiration, though that person was from a humble background.

Bhagaban and Ganesh Samanta were brothers, the latter being the elder one. Bhagaban had been given away in adoption to a relative who lived away from the village. The foster parents had no property worth a mention but made a living out of selling milk and dairy products such as cheese, curd and clarified butter (ghee). Bhagaban's foster parents were distantly related to his mother. They were childless and quite old. They approached Ganesha's parents to give them their second son in adoption. As a child, Ganesha was often ill. An occultist had once told the parents that their second son should have to be given away in adoption for Ganesha to survive.

Bhagaban's parents were very happy when they were approached for the adoption of their son by this relative of theirs. After some initial hesitation, they succumbed to the adoption request. Those days, people held such beliefs and were generally superstitious. Bhagaban's biological parents routinely sent provisions such as paddy to the foster parents, as they were old and unable to work.

Young Bhagaban grew up to be a fine gentleman and his wedding was fixed early in his adolescence. In due course, Bhagaban was blessed with two children—a son and a daughter. After Bhagaban lost his parents (both his own and foster), he decided to return to his ancestral home, but he was not allowed entry by his elder brother. He had already flagged all the property in his name by then.

A row ensued between the two brothers. The elder brother refused to share anything with Bhagaban, who was crestfallen hearing his elder brother's stern words. He had no clue whatsoever as to how to get back his share of the ancestral property. His brother had by then become a wealthy man and enjoyed great influence over fellow villagers. He and his sons were known for using brutal muscle power to resolve conflicts. No one dared to go against Ganesha Samanta. However, after some amount of pleading, luck came Bhagaban's way. Ganesha, counselled by a few influential villagers, relented a bit and allowed the younger brother to stay on the ancestral homestead in the two-roomed outhouse that was once used as a cowshed and a storeroom.

Finding no other way, Bhagaban renovated the shed, cleared the surrounding bushes, marked the borders at a few feet and also cleared a path to the main road. He raised the walls inside the shed too and created three small rooms. He extended the base of the house and made porches. The house was made of mud-mortar with bamboo reinforcement and the roof was made of thatch. He started living there with his wife, son and aunt (his father's sister).

Although the house was still in need of some repair work and demanded regular upkeep, Bhagaban was a happy man. After all, he had a roof over his head. The house was on the other end of the village from where my maternal grandfather's house was located. Bhagaban now lived in peace, if not in abundance. He was loved by one and all in the village for his sunny disposition and sense of courtesy and cordiality. Of course, his own brother always considered Bhagaban a pest and he looked for every opportunity to shoo Bhagaban away from the homestead.

The needs of Bhagaban's family were very minimal: a bowl of rice gruel with edible leaves smothered with a little water, a little mustard oil, a pinch of salt, a little turmeric paste and a few other spices for taste was all that they needed. In terms of clothing, it was the bare minimum: a loin cloth for the men and a simple woven saree for the women.

The women of the house would go to the river bank to collect edible leaves in the early morning. They carried a couple of earthen pots with them which they filled with water needed for cooking and drinking. They did their daily ablutions in the river water. While returning, they would collect dry leaves, twigs and fallen branches from the forest, which were used as fuelwood. And all these would be done before the menfolk woke up.

A portion of the front porch was extended, covered with mud walls on all three sides and a thatch roof built. This was used as the kitchen. Over time, Bhagaban raised a high and thick bamboo fence around his premises, which served two basic purposes: to demarcate his homestead from his elder brother's property and to keep away snakes.

The middle room was used to store provisions and business merchandise. The room to the far end on the east side was used as a bedroom, while the one to the west side was used as a living room. The roof was not very high and was made of thatch that was spread over a framework of split bamboo stalks. The rooms were airy and bright. At night, they used polanga oil lamps with wicks made with cotton rags. This was Bhagaban's home.

Either my paternal grandmother (Bhagaban's wife) or their aunt would smolder a fire in the earthen stove in the kitchen before evening set in and dinner was cooked. My grandmother would take some broken rice from the provisions room and prepare gruel. She would also make some greens curry prepared out of edible leaves that she collected from the river bank. As the meal was being prepared, she would often sit on the porch with her legs stretched out, her husband and his aunt by her side. Their son, too, would sit with them and engage in some leisurely chit-chat.

Soon, Anadi grew up to be handsome, young man. He was a gentleman in the truest sense of the term and had a refined taste for things. There was always a gleam in his eyes—something spiritual about his aura.

Bhagaban liked the smoke from the stove that lingered under the roof of the kitchen. He found contentment in it. He loved his new home, even though it was very modest; the smallest in the village actually. When he stood before it, surveying it, he would tear up and he would feel a great sense of pride. The memories of his parents and of the day he left the house to move in with his foster parents would flash in his mind's eye. He was a very positive person. Whenever he thought about his future, he had no doubt that it would be bright.

'Someday, you will have your own share of ancestral property, your only son will be married and you will get to hear the laughter of your grandchildren. You will have a house with a courtyard for your grandchildren to play in. You will be seated on the porch with your legs stretched out,' his mind would whisper to him.

At sunset, he would sit on the floor of the front porch and stretch his gaze to the western horizon and watch the changing surreal hues of the sky and the sun—from shades of lemon yellow to flaming orange, from red to purple; each colour lending a distinct character to the evening sky. The beauty of these colours would mesmerize him and enchant his heart. Filled with much joy and emotion, he would begin to chant hymns to various gods and goddesses.

Although Bhagaban was happy with his present state of affairs, his share of landholding was not adequate to support his family. He found a few well-wishers in the village who offered him some land for sharecropping. Villagers who didn't own much land resorted to animal husbandry as a way to earn their livelihood; they reared cows on their homestead, prepared ghee and sold them in far-off markets. As there were no roads linking the village to busier markets elsewhere, they would sail on the Paika or walk for miles to areas such as Kujanga, Erasama and so on, to sell their ware. They would also sell their merchandise at the Raghunathpur market, which was some six miles away from Kalarabanka. This market was held on Mondays and Saturdays. Those who had adequate agricultural land earned their livelihood from cultivation.

Coming back to my maternal grandfather's house, pickle-making was one of the most important activities during summer months. Their mango orchards always yielded a bountiful harvest. My grandmother, assisted by maids, would settle down to prepare pickles of various kinds during the summer afternoons. The daughters loved pickles and they also rendered a helping hand with great interest. This was an annual ritual on the homestead.

The maids would cut the green mangoes into different sizes and the children would soak them in home-made brine. The brine-soaked mango pieces would then be taken out and laid on the sunny part of the courtyard to dry. They would then mix an assortment of spices—chopped green chillis, ground red chilli powder, an assortment of other locally available spices, mustard oil, ground mustard, ground cumin seeds and preservatives extracted from other exotic spices—and make a thick paste out of it. The fully dried, chopped green mango pieces, would then be marinated in this spicy slurry and kept in terracotta jars. All these activities were carried out in the second courtyard in the summer afternoons, accompanied by a lot of gossiping and laughter.

My grandfather used to take my grandmother into confidence on important matters relating to family and business. On a Sunday afternoon in the summer of 1942, while the others were busy preparing pickles, Grandfather, who had then just entered the house, summoned Grandmother to the first courtyard. My grandmother, sensing the urgency in his voice, rushed out. She almost leaped from where she was seated, dropping her work then and there and galloped towards the first courtyard. The girls, too, were taken aback. They abruptly stopped their work and scrambled towards the edge of the vestibule that connected the two courtyards and vied for a vantage spot to eavesdrop on the conversation their parents were having.

Sefali's parents stood facing each other, arguing, in the first courtyard.

'Oh, Sefali's mother, I am so happy today. I have found Mr Right for Sefali. Theirs will be the most stunning match,' Grandfather whispered to Grandmother.

'Tell me more about the boy,' Grandmother said, curious to know all about the suitor.

'His name is Anadi, the son of Bhagaban Samanta, who lives on the other side of our village.' Grandfather narrated how he met Anadi and his parents a few days ago and that he had a word with them about Sefali's marriage.

Grandmother didn't quite like the idea. She replied instantly, 'I understand, Nilima's father, and would like to agree with you on this, but I'm afraid I am still apprehensive about the background of the boy. I am surprised that such a wise person as you could take such a hasty decision. Is the boy's future secure? I am a little disappointed. Sefali should be given in marriage to a wealthy boy.'

She paused to gauge my grandfather's reaction. He was listening to her attentively, as he always did. She continued, 'All wealthy people are not bad, are they? There can be loving and caring people in wealthy households, and marrying a wealthy man means that our daughter will sit in the lap of luxury all her life. Wouldn't that be good? Won't you consider looking for a well-to-do boy for your daughter, who is so dear to you?' Her voice trembled as she uttered the last words.

Grandfather was a little flustered over this onslaught from his wife, who hardly ever talked back to him. 'Oh, dear, I appreciate your concern. Money is a useful resource, but I sincerely hope our girls will never feel the need for money too severely, nor be tempted by it. You have groomed them so well and I am grateful for that,' he insisted.

Grandfather was hopeful and asserted that Anadi would soon be established in his business, earning enough for a good living and that their daughter will be comfortable. He would under no circumstances let go of this perfect match. He would be quite content to see Nilimarani begin humbly, for if he was not mistaken, she would be rich in the possession of a good man's heart, and that was better than a fortune. My grandmother was taken aback at Grandfather's firm stand, but she chose to plead with him again. 'I will appreciate it if you give her hand in marriage to a loving, caring and handsome boy belonging to an affluent family.'

'If rank and money came with love and virtue, I would accept them gracefully, but I know from experience, that genuine happiness can be found in a plain little house too, where daily bread is earned through sweat and toil. She will be rich in that she will have the love and admiration of a good man, and to me, that is more important than having a big fortune.'

Though the conversation lasted for only a few minutes, to the girls it felt like it stretched for hours. My grandmother couldn't find anything else to say. She turned and walked away towards the inner courtyard, where she perched herself on the east-facing porch. Her face had unusually reddened and she looked thoughtful and tensed.

As she took deep breaths, she signalled the maids to call it a day. The girls too were asked to collect the ingredients in bamboo trays and take them to the dining room, to be taken out for drying the next afternoon.

'What is it, Mother? You look very tense!' asked Sefali, taking the lead, while the two younger daughters clutched at her saree. Grandmother's face was flushed and swollen, her vision blurry. She looked up towards the cloudless sky, trying to hide her anguish. There was silence, a silence fraught with tension and fear of what was to come. Grandmother then lowered her head, took a deep breath and in a rather sullen voice, said to her daughter, 'Some people will be coming tomorrow to see you. They intend to ask your hand in marriage for their son, if they like you at all.'

Sefali was shocked at this sudden revelation. The weather within her changed, from glee to gloom, in an instant. She had just stepped into her fifteenth year. She couldn't believe her ears, yet she didn't have the courage to ask her mother to repeat what she had just said. 'What? Marry me? Should I laugh or should I cry? Is this a joke, Mother?'

She looked completely flustered. 'Why are girls considered a bundle of misery and a burden when they grow up and then let off in marriage before they can even understand the meaning and implication of a marriage? Why do girls have to leave their homes and go to stay with their in-laws after marriage? Why are such tormenting norms imposed on girls?' she thought to herself.

Her thoughts became hazy as she began imagining what was to follow in her life. Silence fell upon all—a silence afflicted by helplessness and a simmering anger of revolt. Sefali was furious. She puffed and huffed like a wild bull as she romped around the courtyard in total bewilderment. The younger children looked at her in total consternation. Everybody was speechless. She decided to raise her voice against the marriage proposal. She lowered her head, tears still rolling down her cheeks. She took a deep breath and uttered a faint protest, 'Mother, no...'

'But your "no" is not taken into consideration, dear, rather, can't be taken into consideration. You better understand this. Sooner or later, you *will* have to be let off in marriage. I feel for you and understand the reason for your objection. We know that you are very young for marriage, but we cannot go by what our hearts dictate. We have to consider the social norms that have been in place for generations. The real house of a woman is her husband's. For everything, there is a reason and there is a season. Your future in-laws will be here to see you tomorrow.'

Sefali knew her mother. When she made up her mind, it was difficult to convince her otherwise. She pleaded again, 'Mother, I'm only fifteen. How can you think of marrying me off now? What do I know about marriage? I still love playing in the garden. I still love playing hopscotch. I still long to go into the orchards and pluck seasonal fruits. No, I am not as mature as you are. Please...'

Her mother heard her out but chided, 'Shame, shame, Sefali, how can you speak like that; that's rather unbecoming of you. You are ridiculing all the grooming that we have given you with such dedication, aren't you?'

When she saw Sefali's stance beaming with total resentment, she said with a heavy voice, 'Your marriage is not going to happen tomorrow. So, you needn't worry about it now. In our culture, once the wedding is fixed, your objection to it will be held as abominable vulgarity and you will be seen by society as having thrown yourself away to waste. For generations, not a single girl in our society has ever questioned this tradition, and no daughter of mine is going to be the one to start either. Your opinion does not matter. At your age, girls are seen holding their babies in their laps.'

My grandmother was done talking, but my mother wasn't convinced. She walked to the farther end of the courtyard, sat on the edge of the porch, with her head lowered. After a couple of seconds, she looked up. Her beautiful inky eyes were now dull and glossy with unshed tears; there were no spark in them anymore. All that her eyes showed was hurt, anger, disgust and hatred. She closed her eyes and a tear trickled down. Her heart was broken. She covered her face in her palms and broke into sobs. For Sefali's tender and fragile mind, these sudden developments were like a nightmare and she was not able to handle them. She did have a premonition that the days of her freedom were drawing to a close and that she would soon be put in a cage. She was unable to reconcile to the fact that she could not voice her resistance. She knew that she was helpless, just as much as her mother. She would eventually have to bow down to the decision of the male-dominated society and her voice crushed.

Sefali's teenage mind was scurrying for support. She rushed to her father's room. Her breaths shortened and she looked frightened. An uncomfortable silence prevailed around her. She wrung her hands. Time ticked slowly. She paused at the threshold of the room with her head lowered. She peeped into the room to assess her father's mood. He was reading. She contemplated barging in and asking her father right away if what she had heard was true. 'But that will be rude,' her judicious sense prevailed and she stopped. Bringing her palms together in the Namaskar Mudra, she looked away, and prayed silently, 'Oh, how I wish what my mother just said was a joke or a mistake.' She returned to the porch facing her father's room and began scratching the floor of the courtyard with her toenails.

Darkness was beginning to spread its wings over the courtyard. She waited. My grandfather's eyes were still glued to the document he was reading. It had been quite some time now. Her face grew pale. She turned her gaze towards the auspicious holy basil plant and prayed silently, 'Goddess Mother, why should girls have to go through all this? You are a woman, too. Please help me.'

She turned her gaze towards the room but could not gather enough courage to question her father. 'No, I can't face him. What will I tell him? What will I ask him?' She decided retrace her steps to the kids' room in the second block. She was just about to turn, when she heard her father's voice. 'Is there anything that is bothering you, sweetheart? Come in and spit it out without hesitation.'

Sefali looked at her father, hopeful. She trudged across the courtyard, into her father's room and stood in his front of him, her head lowered and her gaze fixed on her toes. She was sobbing. An awkward silence fell between them. Seeing her hesitation, he again coaxed her to speak forth. He perhaps knew that she had come to talk about the marriage proposal. Being a wise man, he knew his responsibilities as a father and as a member of the society and the consequences of not being able to carry them out. 'I assume your mother has already spoken to you. I can understand what you are going through.'

Sefali faintly uttered, 'But...'

However, before she could finish or rather begin to speak, Grandfather interrupted her, 'Well, your emotions are but natural. They will melt away once you get married. You will have a happy married life and a good family. I assure you that the boy I have chosen for you is one who has no match in seven villages with regard to his looks and mannerism. You will make a great pair.'

Hearing these words, my mother ran back to her room and locked herself inside. She sat in a corner with her head perched on her knees and began sobbing inconsolably.

My grandmother had already assessed the emotional turmoil that Sefali was undergoing. She requested her neighbour's newlyweds daughter-in-law, who was a little over eighteen years, to come and comfort Sefali. Sefali was fond of her and lovingly addressed her as 'bhauja' (sister-in-law). They had struck an amiable equation with each other in their first meeting. They cracked jokes and played Ludo during the afternoons.

On seeing Sefali's sad face, she tickled her to make her laugh, 'Wait till you have someone to throw his arms around you and say "I love you". He will be your sunshine. We will be outsiders. You will be on your own, you will find a shoulder to lean on. Oh, darling, sing to him his favourite melody, speak to him from your heart. Curl on him like a creeper with pink and amber blossoms till he whispers in your ears, "I want so much." Give him a touch of your magic senses, so he falls asleep, as if he smelt the fragrance of a thousand jasmines.' These words from her friend made Sefali smile and lightened the mood. At that time, she felt guilty for blurting out such stern words at her mother. But then she was still upset with her. How could she? How could she wear that stony veil on her face and hurl those stern words at her?

The next day, as was scheduled by Grandfather, Anadi's father and a couple of his well-wishers arrived at Sefali's house. Grandfather received the guests at the front gate and ushered them to the living room. Then, he scurried up to the middle block and upon entering the room where Sefali was getting ready, he said, 'Listen, Sefali's mother, they are here! We must see that they are well treated. We have only three guests, including Anadi's father.' He deliberately shared this information with Grandmother in the presence of my mother, so that she too could prepare herself accordingly.

That morning, Grandmother had woken up very early. She quickly tidied up the house and went into the kitchen after her morning ablutions. The entire morning, she was busy making a range of sweetmeats for the visitors. Directed by her mother, Sefali woke up early, performed her morning ablutions and joined her in the kitchen. While they were working in the kitchen, my grandmother advised my mother on how to behave in front of her prospective in-laws. Grandmother even took out the time to help her daughter get ready for the special day. My mother's dark hair was oiled and done in a neat braid, which complemented her beautiful features and fair complexion. She even accessorized her hair with some fresh flowers. Her hands and feet were decorated with alta, a red dye. It was customary to dress in a simple but traditional attire (usually, a silk saree) for such occasions. So, my mother wore one of my grandmother's expensive, handwoven silk sarees—an orange one with maroon borders and delicate floral motifs. The orange colour of the saree was like that of the early morning sun—vibrant and gorgeous. She outlined her lower and upper eyelids with home-made kajal.

When my mother was ready, my grandmother became quite emotional. My little girl is all grown up and ready to leave us for a new life, she thought to herself. Tears rolled down her cheeks and she quickly turned her face away and wiped them with the free end of her saree. Poor Sefali's heart was pounding with anxiety. This was the toughest part in a girl's life—a big transition.

When the guests were seated in the living room, Grandmother stood a little away from the threshold, making sure they couldn't see her. Her gaze followed Sefali as she walked towards the living room. 'Ah, bless my little soul, she looks so beautiful!' Grandmother mused, pleased. She felt proud of her daughter as she retreated to her room, waiting anxiously for Sefali's return.

The ambience in the living room was tranquil, but it failed to calm my mother's nerves. She had clung to her mother's hand firmly as she was escorted to the living room. Please let this be over soon, Sefali said a silent prayer.

Having stepped inside the room, she halted a little farther from the doorstep. She involuntarily locked her palms together—a gesture of submission and respect towards elders. With a flame raging inside her, she stood there for what seemed like an eternity. She felt lonely even with the people around. Then, she heard her father introducing her to the visitors. He gestured her to pay her customary reverence to the guests.

Sefali walked slowly and gracefully to each of the visitor. Kneeling down, she bowed before them, including her father. Everybody blessed her. After the initial introductions and pleasantries were exchanged, she stood in the centre of the room, waiting for further instructions. Though unhappy with the proceedings, she stood like a lamp post, right in the middle of the room. Her head was lowered and she kept staring at her toes.

Soon, her younger sisters came into the living room carrying trays of pitha and other delicacies and placed them on the rug in front of the guests. Their presence in the room gave Sefali some comfort of company. However, they returned soon after laying the plates and bowls of sweetmeats. The guests were offered yogurt, rasgulla, chakuli pitha and an assortment of fresh seasonal fruits, including ripe bananas and mangoes.

Sefali unwittingly looked towards the garden. Oh, how I will miss your lap when I am gone from here to my in-laws' house, she thought to herself. She felt an urgent urge to run to the garden, a place that was so dear to her.

Then, my grandfather looked at the guests. 'Well...' he said, his voice laced with optimism and hope that the marriage proposal will be accepted. After all, it was an agreement made between the heads of the two families. However, silence prevailed. Such meetings were usually awkward. The guests looked at each other. My mother, too, stole a glance at the guests; their expressions vague. The deafening and awkward silence was broken when one of the guests cleared his throat and began preparing to make a speech, perhaps unable to take the silence any longer. They scrutinized her, again. She was unable to read their thoughts. She was flushed with anxiety and embarrassment. Suddenly, she heard someone addressing her, 'Nilima, you may go now. You have our earnest blessings!' She bowed before the guests once again and took their leave. One of the guests, an elderly, known to both the heads of the families, spoke very gently, 'They will make a perfect couple. They are made for each other.' Everyone nodded their heads in agreement, smiling.

Once out of the room, Sefali pulled the loose end of her saree and dabbed the perspiration off her face. 'Oh, poor you, how awkward was that! What a dreadful afternoon! You haven't been this nervous ever! Thank God, the meeting was over sooner than expected!' she heard her inner voice comfort her.

When she was back in her room, Sefali spread a straw mat on the floor and sat at a corner, her back leaning against the wall and her face buried in her palms. She was anxious with an unexplainable rage. She wanted to stomp her feet, scream, give her mother a good shaking, cry. She didn't know how else to express what she was feeling. But she couldn't do any of that. Exhausted, she drifted into a deep slumber.

It was already sunset when the visitors left. Grandfather also went out after the visitors. Later in the evening, my grandmother came into the room after offering her ritualistic ovations at the feet of the holy basil plant. She sat by Sefali's side and laid a comforting hand on her head and lovingly caressed her silky hair. My mother woke up with a jerk. Her gaze was blazing with anguish when they met her mother's gaze.

'Well, won't you want your fortune told?' her mother asked, her voice as decisive as always, but as soft as her beautiful features.

'I don't care, Mother,' she said rather rudely.

There was silence for a while. Both mother and daughter kept gauging each other. Sefali softened her stance, realizing her rude behaviour. 'You may if it will please you.'

'It's your usual impudence again. I knew how you would react. I heard it from your footsteps as you crossed the threshold of this room and went inside.'

'Oh, did you?' Sefali's reaction was very close to being violent.

'Yes, I did. I have a sharp eye and a good brain. You, too, will need these to be a good wife and a homemaker.'

Sefali turned her face away. She was in a terrible mood. She didn't care for anything in the world. She cursed her fate and fell onto the bed with her face in her palms and began to sob.

'Come on, Sefali, my darling, the wedding is not happening tomorrow. It will probably happen in a year's time. Your father and I have talked it over. Your future in-laws have also agreed that the wedding can wait for a couple of years, as you both are very young now. Very understanding people indeed. Cheer up, my child!'

Sefali was relieved when she heard that. Her body that was stiff with tension, slowly began to relax. She jumped out of bed and flung her arms around her mother, who took her in a tight embrace.

Then, her mother spoke softly, 'You are charming and beautiful, my child. You are young and full of life. You are endowed with the gifts of class and good fortune. I'm sure the boy your father has chosen for you will be to your best liking. He is from our village and has a decent background. He is sober and handsome. Your father knows what's best for you. You will be happy with him. You will make a fine wife too.'

In the spring of 1943, the wedding of Nilimarani and Anadi Samanta was solemnized. She was sixteen then and her spouse was eight years older to her.

4

ANADI AND NILIMARANI

The morning after the wedding, the newlyweds began making preparations for their journey to the groom's house. My mother's relatives, friends and neighbours gathered to give the couple a warm and affectionate send-off. After the ceremonial rituals, the bride and the groom had to kneel down, bow at the feet of their parents, take the dust off their feet as blessings and smear them on their foreheads.

Tendrils of the golden morning sunlight seeped through the swinging fronds of coconut and areca nut palm trees as the newlyweds made their way to the front garden. The couple was led out by the bride's parents to a beautifully decorated bullock-cart. The morning was soothingly breezy and the trees were swaying to the beats of the music played by a country band near the cart.

With a heavy heart, my mother started making her way towards her new home. This homestead, which had cradled her for sixteen-long years, would no longer be hers. She wouldn't be referring to it as 'my house' anymore. Her world was going to change forever.

Just the other day, she was a toddler and in the blink of an eye, this angel had blossomed into a beautiful young girl. Just the other day, her wedding was being fixed and today she was standing at the threshold of a new life, without her parents. She was going to live with a stranger in *his* house.

While parting, it was customary for the bride to throw fistfuls of rice behind her, without looking back. This was an expression of the fact that that house was no longer the girl's and she was leaving everything behind. As they were on their way out, the couple crossed the garden which was Nilimarani's favourite place in the house. She paused near the shrub that bore fragrant white flowers, one of her very favourite flowers. She plucked a handful and scattered them on the ground, kneeling and pressing her cheek against the soft grass.

While bidding her farewell, Sefali's mother took her in a warm embrace. 'My dear daughter, I can understand what you are going through. But soon, you will forget this pain. You will seek your husband at every step of your life. You will encourage him and use your love to rescue him if things go downhill. Never turn your back on him. Like water, like breath and like raindrops on the earth, you will mould yourself in him and enjoy freedom in each other's arms. That's how you will find bliss of marital life, my dear. The foundation of a lasting relationship between husband and wife essentially lies in unconditional love and friendship.'

Sefali put her head on her mother's shoulder and began to sob. Her father came from behind and led her to the coach. It was customary for a bride's brother to accompany her on the journey to her new home for the first time, but since Sefali did not have a brother, their neighbour's son accompanied her.

The ride seemed long and awkward. My mother sat with her legs folded at the knees while her veiled head rested on the knees. There was complete silence inside the carriage, except for the continuous rattling of the wheels as the cart made its way across the rough village terrain. Occasionally, some village urchins would yell cheerfully, waving their hands, 'There goes the bride! There goes the bride!' The happy and carefree laughter of the children made her feel a little better.

Since the groom's family lived in the same village, it did not take them very long to reach. When the carriage reached the groom's house, a band began playing wedding songs, the women blew conches and they made the traditional crooning sound with their mouths to ward off evil spirits. Nilimarani's mother-in-law, accompanied by a bevy of women, helped the newlyweds get down from the cart. With a big smile, she hugged Nilimarani and kissed her on the forehead. Scanning her new daughter-in-law from tip to toe, she chirped, 'You look beautiful, dear!' Then, she turned to Anadi and hugged him as well. 'My baby boy has become a young man,' she cooed. 'Oh no, not again, Mother! Why do you always have to say that?' he feigned a mild protest. She smiled and pulled his cheeks. She ushered the couple into the house. They received a very warm welcome amidst a lot of merrymaking. Nilimarani had stopped sobbing by then. She even sneaked a glance at Anadi from under the corner of her veil. He was handsome, with thick black curls. Though he was fair, his hands and face were somewhat tanned and weather-beaten. Probably from working in the field all day, my mother thought to herself. He was very quiet throughout the function.

When the rituals and merrymaking drew to a close, Nilimarani's mother-in-law addressed them, 'Be nice to each other. Try to be friends first, and see where that takes you. Relationships aren't built in a day, it takes time. Be patient and respect each other. Bless you!' The couple bowed and touched her feet.

Soon, the bride and groom retired to the innermost room, where they were served sweetmeats. The room was decorated with fresh flowers, the beautiful fragrance of the blossoms heavy in the air. My mother sat with her face still covered by the veil. It was customary for the bride to refrain from doing any household work for a week after the wedding. A few girls from the neighbourhood, most of them younger than Nilimarani, were called to help them out when needed. Most of these girls, young and carefree, cracked jokes and narrated hilarious anecdotes. My mother didn't find herself alone as she had apprehended. From time to time, women from the neighborhood would come in to pay a visit, too. The happy atmosphere relaxed my mother's frayed nerves and made her feel at home.

Nilimarani, with her bright disposition, gelled well with the family. Her smile had no rival. She usually had visitors from the neighbourhood during the late-afternoon. She gleefully recounted the conversations she had with them to her husband.

Even after a week of the wedding, the house was filled with relatives and neighbours. Just before the wedding ceremony, the walls of the house were painted with murals and motifs in red, white and yellow colours. Flowers of different hues, shapes and sizes decorated the doors, windows and even the walls. The house was airy and sunny. Flowery fragrance pervaded the atmosphere inside the rooms. My father used to crave for some time alone with my mother so that he could talk to her in private and get to know her better. Unfortunately, she was always surrounded by people. At night, they would just go off to sleep, as even a whisper drifted to the first room, where my paternal grandmother and aunt slept.

One evening, when my mother was resting, my father came in and announced that an elderly lady would soon be visiting to bless her. He asked her to freshen up and make herself presentable. When the guest arrived, she was ushered into my mother's room. My mother's aunt-in-law took some sweets from the sweetmeat basket, brought by my mother with her from her parents' house and served the elderly lady. It was tradition. No sooner did the visitor leave that my father flung the door open and bounced into their room, grinning. It was evening and the young girls had already left for the day. My mother was alone in the room. She glanced at him as he squatted on the floor, right in front of her. Her heart skipped a beat. My mother quickly pulled her veil to partially cover her head and face. He was thinking of initiating a conversation with her but every time he tried, he found himself at a loss for words.

'I'm glad you're having fun,' he said finally, breaking the awkward silence, his lips sculpted into a loving smile, 'I don't know what the lady told you; though, upon my honour, I tried not to hear, but I did catch some of her words. She praised your beauty and remarkable manners. She is genuine. Let me be the first to congratulate you. You left a splendid impression on her. She is the oldest woman in the neighbourhood and is well regarded by one and all. You know what, she is quite taken by your grace and manners and that fills me with immense pride. I entirely agree with her. I have never been happier in my entire life. You really fascinate me.' That was the first conversation my parents had. Then a tormenting silence prevailed between them and moments ticked by. Anadi was quite tense. He had never come this close to any girl in his life so far. He could see the outline of her face from behind the veil. She looked lovely, but he was perplexed and intrigued. Will she give me a reply, he thought to himself.

My mother looked up from behind the veil. Her husband's compliments pleased her. She stared at him for a second. She wanted to burst out into a peal of laughter at his eagerness, but restrained herself and pulled the veil so as to cover her face. 'Thank you, sir.' She managed to put together a reply, all the while suppressing a giggle.

My father continued, 'She is very caring and of good nature. Very few people are so compassionate.'

She blushed and let out a faint smile, rich and genuine.

He quickly added, 'I hope you are finding it pleasant here. Is there anything you need? Please do tell.'

She lifted her head. Looking at his face, she said, 'Oh, it's quite okay here, don't you worry at all.'

Anadi found Nilimarani to be very charming and he planned his day around her schedule in the hope of catching a fleeting glimpse of her. He was so attracted to her that he was almost flummoxed by her very existence. She was like a rainbow and she filled his life with beautiful colours. Her colourful attire competed with her bright jangling bangles. He wanted to know everything about her—her favourite food, what she fancied doing in her spare time and everything about her opulent life before marriage.

According to tradition, on the eighth day after the wedding, my parents returned to my mother's parental home. It was a day of jollity for the entire family. Grandfather had invited the whole village to join the newlyweds for lunch. The couple returned to the groom's house the next morning.

The mutual attachment between Anadi and Nilimarani was beginning to grow. Both had begun admiring each other. Nilimarani began to realize what her father meant when he had once said: 'I understand your anxiety, but I'm sure they will melt away as soon you meet him. You will have a happy life with him. I assure you that you both will make a good match.' She knew his words were coming true.

However, she was initially shocked when she saw her husband's house—it was a very small one, almost like a hut; and there was not enough space for ten people even. She remembered her mother's parting words and learnt to take it all in her stride. She started to help out her mother-in-law and aunt-in-law in the household chores, including cooking.

Days turned into weeks and weeks into months. My father's days were no longer planned around my mother's activities, as was the case earlier. He worked at home for a few days before going out on his usual business trips. Nilimarani saw very little of her husband during those days. Whatever little time she had with him, she cherished it and it made her comfortable in the new set-up. She started to mingle with the rest of family. She was her own self again, regaining her confidence. She found him to be the perfect gentleman—as she had imagined. Above all, she hoped to find in him a pleasant companion. All in all, she had started to like him.

Soon, she got to know the other members of the household, about their lives and their concerns. He told her how his paternal uncle had usurped the ancestral property and how they had all come to stay in this small house. He also spoke about his business and prospects at length. Within a few weeks, he became her biggest confidant.

My mother's in-laws were very loving and quite broad-minded; she was made to feel like a daughter. Her aunt-in-law loved to comb her hair every morning and evening; she would do my mother's hair in a low bun and decorate it with flowers. Then, she would take her time to admire my mother's beauty and not hesitate to plant a kiss on her forehead. She would often look up at the sky and thank Mother Durga for bestowing them with this angel as their daughter-in-law.

My mother was content and happy in her new house, with her new family. She enjoyed the same kind of freedom at her new home as she did at her parents'. Soon, she became the darling of the neighbourhood. She would leisurely wander from house to house in the afternoon, accompanied by her mother-in-law or aunt-in-law. My mother was not expected to be behind a veil all the time. She kept it partially on when she came upon elders.

My mother helped my father prepare clarified butter, which he sold in far-away markets. When my father was at home, my mother would study with him. His innocence and commitment towards work was indeed admirable. On weekdays, he would set out early in the morning and return by evening. Nilimarani always waited eagerly for his return. She would stand at the threshold to welcome him. When back home in the evening, my father would sit on the porch—his legs dangling over the edge. The whole family usually sat together on the porch in the evenings. They would all listen with rapt attention to Anadi's account of the business proceedings of the week.

Anadi was aware of Nilimarani's affluence and always feared that she was disappointed, given his financial condition. I brought home such a young girl as a bride. Perhaps she dreamt of a better life and a better companion. Am I ruining her life, or am I helping her to blossom? These questions often troubled him.

One morning, as he took a break from their work, he ventured out to ask her, 'Nilima, do you believe in the power of thoughts?'

'What's that? I am not aware of it,' She said, nodding her head.

'Our thoughts are very powerful. They, in a way, define us, our life. Our thoughts become our truth. We attract into our lives what we believe and that, my dear, is the influence of our thoughts. You come from a very affluent family and our lifestyle and upbringing don't match. It hurts me seeing you pulled out of your comfortable homestead and dropped into this dingy house.'

During the final weeks before their wedding, she was taught by her mother to make a house a home. She had learned to find the finer nuances in her mother's dexterous handling of the house. Every night, as she lay in bed, she tried to visualize the life that was awaiting her, she tried to think about the new place that she would have to call 'home'. At times, bright colours filled her mind; at others, darkness blurred everything around her. Her dreams as well as her nightmares kept her awake.

'I have no intention of hankering after material assets. I'm more than content with whatever little we have here and I will never be ashamed or embarrassed about what we don't have,' said Nilimarani and she meant what she said.

She was quite hurt by this question, but her reply took a big load off her husband's troubled mind. He felt lighter. 'I am sorry. I shouldn't have made you uncomfortable. Perhaps, there is a reason why we are drawn to each other,' Anadi said, apologetically. He smiled and there was a sparkle in his eyes.

'It's okay, we shall not talk about this ever again,' she sighed and gave him a faint but warm smile.

He opened his mouth, as if to say something, but chose not to. His words left her thinking and also made her heart melt. She realized how good a person he was and resolved to stand by him, no matter what.

The advent of the twentieth century was remarkable in terms of development, with the establishment of India's first-ever integrated steel plant at Kalimati in Mayurbhanj district of Odisha by a budding entrepreneur from western India, Jamsetji Tata. A beautiful, modern township was developed around the factory and named Jamshedpur. In 1910, the Bengal–Nagpur Railways established a railway station on the Howrah–Bombay route at Kalimati, which was near Sakchi, the location of the steel plant. The township was connected to the city of Bombay (now Mumbai) on the western coast, and Howrah and Kharagpur junctions on the south-eastern coast. The railways was the lifeline of the steel plant. The name of the railway station was later changed to Tatanagar, in honour of its founder, Jamsetji Tata. As time progressed, more and more people from the nearby areas and even far-off places such as West Bengal, Tamil Nadu and Kerala began migrating to Tatanagar (also called Jamshedpur) in search of jobs.

Many young boys left the comfort of their homes and came to this new town for jobs in Tata Company. My father too was considering relocating to Jamshedpur. A friend of his who was already working in Tata Company was visiting the village at that time. He came to see my father and it was he who suggested that my father go with him to Tatanagar, where he would help him find a job.

'Such a wonderful opportunity!' thought Anadi to himself. 'Nilima is indeed my lady-luck!'

That evening as the whole family sat on the front porch, my father suggested the idea of moving to Jamshedpur for the first time.

'What do you mean?' His mother yelled from the kitchen.

'Hush. Don't let the neighbours hear about it.'

'So you want to go to Tatanagar in pursuit of a better life? I have heard that life is a lot better there. You have a long life ahead of you. Getting a job in the company will serve you well. I have heard that they pay well and provide a house, too. So when do you plan to leave?' my grandfather asked.

Anadi did not expect such a positive response from his father. He was delighted.

'In a week's time. I will have to go with my friend, who is already working in the company. He has assured that he will help me land a job.'

'You need to establish yourself in a career of your own choice. I will not be a hindrance howsoever. I wish you well. Always be mindful and don't be extravagant, as you have to look after us as well as your new family. You always have been a man with good sense and admirable conduct. Let your forbearance and countenance be not wasted in a strange land. Rise and shine, my son!' his father's blessing were soulful.

A faint smile appeared on Anadi's lips while his mother, aunt and wife looked flabbergasted. Hugging his mother and aunt, my father said, 'Don't worry, I will be back soon. Bless me!'

'Goddess Mother Durga be with you always, dear!' They blessed my father.

Anadi was soon employed in Tata Company as a workman. Since he was not in a high post, he was not provided with any quarter. Initially, he lived with his friend. He was not even allowed to take leave for six months. After the probation period, he visited his village for a couple of days.

When Anadi was away in Jamshedpur, Nilimarani's parents realized that she might start feeling lonely. Those days, it was not common for a girl's parents to visit her at her husband's house. A girl's parents eschewed visiting their daughter until she delivered an heir. But since my father and mother were from the same village, my mother would visit her home almost every weekend. When my mother came back to her in-laws' house, my maternal grandmother would send with her a sack full of rice, vegetables, coconuts and other useful provisions, including hairpins, hairclips, coconut oil and kajal. This was tradition and my grandparents insisted on following it. If on some weekend, Nilimarani couldn't go to her parents' house, they would visit her instead and customarily bring with them the sack full of provisions.

One fine morning, in the summer of 1950, my parents set out for Tatanagar to start a new life together, all by themselves.

'It is nice to see a bit more of the world,' Nilimarani observed.

Not too long ago, she had left her parents' house. In a bullock cart, she was sent off from the home where she was born and raised in. A young girl, still in her teens, had travelled across the village, sad and heartbroken at being separated from her family and blood relations. Then she had to leave her in-laws' home. She was starting a new chapter of her life with her partner, her husband—for good or for worse.

They were given a tearful send-off. The road to Cuttack, the gateway to the outside world for the Odias living in the coastal belt, was the same as it was decades before. My parents travelled to the Cuttack railway station in my grandfather's bullock cart. After a four-hour ride on a bumpy track, they reached the station. It was Nilimarani's first-ever trip out of the village. She had goosebumps at the prospect of exploring a new life beyond the village, and undeniably, not many were as lucky as my mother.

There was no direct train to Tatanagar. They had to change trains at the Kharagpur railway junction. The train journey was a once-in-a-lifetime experience for Nilimarani, again something very few women in the village had the good fortune of experiencing. Being at the railway station was a new and pleasant experience in itself. The multitude of people, the hustle and bustle—it was all very new to her. The sight of the trains approaching and entering the platform was a bit scary for her. The deafening rattling and screeching of the train's wheels as the train came to a halt, the cloud of sooty smoke belching up and rising in the sky, the 'chug chug' sound it made—everything was new and fascinating to the twenty-one-year-old Nilimarani. Her experience at the Kharagpur railway junction, the biggest railway junction on the south-eastern section of the Indian Railways, was more thrilling.

As the train pulled out of the Cuttack station, the thrilled Nilimarani, who had secured a window seat by now, stretched her hand out of the window and began enjoying the rush of the wind. Soon, it was pitch dark and nothing outside was visible. Tired and sleepy, she rested her head on her husband's shoulder and slipped into a peaceful sleep.

The couple deboarded at the Kharagpur station at about three o'clock the next morning. They had to wait for two hours at the platform for the next connecting train to come in. The journey to Jamshedpur was long despite the fact that the train was moving at a rapid speed. Soon, it started to rain. At dawn, the sun was out on the eastern horizon, beaming with its orange rays through the light clouds. It was an extraordinary experience for Nilimarani. She closed her eyes and took a deep breath—as if trying to take in the scenic beauty in its entirety.

Suddenly, her mind drifted to her parental homestead and the image of her mother flashed in her mind. Not too long back, at the age of twenty-one, she had gone through the most painful experience of her life—that of losing her mother. After she lost her mother to illness, she was given the responsibility of taking care of her very young brother.

'What are you thinking?' asked Anadi, who was looking at Nilimarani as she continued looking out of the window, lost in thought. He noticed a tear roll down her eye.

'I don't know why, but suddenly, the memories of Mother's death flashed in my mind. I can't stop the tears and the ache in my heart. I yearn to be with her again. I... I want to feel her love and comforting touch again...' she choked as the heart-rending scenes of that fateful night flashed in her mind's eye. Anadi, who understood her feelings and what she was going through, consoled her.

Her mother was Nilimarani's most faithful companion and confidante. She, being the firstborn, was the most loved and pampered. Her mother dedicated her life to caring for her children, physically and emotionally. She always seemed to know when to be tough with the children and when to be soft, how to help them to overcome their problems and how to thrive in spite of them. Her mother's love was irreplaceable, which made losing her a very painful experience. While

Nilimarani carried in her heart a lasting ache, she continued searching for the happiness her mother had always wished and hoped for her.

Two years into Nilimarani's marriage, her two sisters, too, were married off in quick succession. Her parents were blessed with a boy during that time. Nilimarani was very happy and thankful to her mother for giving her a brother and she cared for him like a mother. During that time, their mother was taken ill and the cause of her illness couldn't be diagnosed. A few months after childbirth, her mother was almost bedridden and her condition deteriorated. Nilimarani often visited her parents during that time to look after her baby brother and her ailing mother, as her father would be in Raghunathpur on work. She would spend the day at her parents' and then return home in the afternoon, after her father was back. This was a routine for almost three months.

One day, her mother's situation suddenly worsened and Nilimarani was summoned by her father. On reaching her house, she rushed to her mother's bedroom. She found her mother to be very weak and frail; she looked extremely pale too and her hair, unkempt. She moaned in pain, in a barely audible voice.

'How are you feeling, Mother?' asked Nilimarani as she begun caressing her legs.

'A little weak to...today...' her mother stuttered. The effort to speak made her breathless.

Nilimarani felt a tingle of anxiety and helplessness. Her mother took to bed just a few months after delivery. It started as joint pains. Soon, she was too weak to do anything on her own. The previous week, she had contracted a cold and now, she was running a fever and having trouble breathing.

'Is there anything you need?' Nilimarani asked.

Her mother wasn't eating well for the past few days and was sinking with each passing day.

'No.'

Nilimarani repeated the question, and every time, she got the same reply.

'Should I ask Father to fetch the vaidya?' Nilimarani asked her mother, worried. The vaidya had given her an extract of poppies mixed in honey and alcohol that brought some comfort and relief.

'No, dear,' her mother said in a tone that revealed the pain she was going through. Despite that, she asked, 'How is everything at home? How is everyone?'

'Everybody is alright. Fine people they are, Mother. I am happy there. Don't you worry. In fact, Father-in-law insists on me coming here every day to look after you and my little brother. I am going to stay here now till you get well enough to be on your own again.' Nilimarani noticed her mother's lips—they were very pale, almost black—and she was terrified.

Nilimarani's mother took a pause to catch her breath, and then asked her, 'What did you do this morning?'

'Oh, nothing much! Mother-in-law and Aunt-in-law will not let me cut a strand of straw even. "Go and see your mother," Mother-in-law had urged this morning. "Maybe your presence will cheer her up," she had said. They have asked me to stay here till you get better, Mother.'

Her mother's illness was unnerving, everything was uncertain at that time. They all feared the inevitable. That day, when the sun was about to set, Nilimarani's father called her and asked, 'Do you want to return to your in-laws' homestead?'

'No, Father, I should stay here with Mother till she gets better; that is my mother-in-law's order.'

Father looked happy. 'I know they are good souls.'

Nilimarani went to the kitchen and prepared some tapioca porridge for her mother, that's what she ate for meals. A woman from the neighbourhood came twice a day—in the morning and in the evening—to cook. Her two married sisters, who were in the same village, would also take turns to come and look after their mother. Nilimarani took charge of the house besides attending to her mother and brother.

The next day, her father fetched the vaidya. As he checked her mother's condition, Nilimarani asked him, 'Will Goddess Mother make my mother better?'

Her father raised his eyebrows and looked at her questioningly.

Such a direct question, he thought to himself. 'Everyone is praying for her recovery, my dear!'

The vaidya, after checking Grandmother, said that he would prepare another potion, which should relieve her from pain and bring down the fever, too.

Two days later, the vaidya was summoned again. He checked my grandmother's pulse, listened to her heartbeat, checked her pupils, checked the joints and examined her breath. He then sank into a thoughtful countenance and looked away from her. He looked at her again.

'What are you going to do, doctor?' Nilimarani was anxious to know about the next course of action.

The vaidya looked up at Nilimarani, a strange concern shrouded his eyes.

She, however, felt a surge of hope rising inside her. 'Will my mother be alright?' she asked.

The doctor didn't respond and turned his gaze away instead. He looked at her father. 'Please ask your daughter to go out of the room. I want a moment alone with you, sir. It is about your wife's health.'

Nilimarani went out of the room but didn't go too far. She stood near the door from where she could overhear the one-sided conversation. Her father didn't say a word. 'Sir, your wife's health is sinking very fast. Her condition is critical.'

Nilimarani's father's eyes were moist. A couple of teardrops hung at the corner of his eyes. Wiping away his tears, he asked, 'Doctor, can't you do anything? Maybe try some other potion...'

'Sir, please hold yourself together and allow me to be honest; your wife is...err ...err...dying. She may not make it through this night unless some miracle happens... God bless her soul, pray for her, please pray for her...' the vaidya could speak no more.

Her father's stomach began to wrench. Nilimarani couldn't hold back her tears. Oh Goddess Mother, please save my mother! she prayed.

That night, neither Nilimarani's mother nor her father could sleep. She slept by her mother's side, frequently getting up to check on her. She tried feeding her a spoonful of barley gruel and made her drink some water at regular intervals.

Grandfather, too, sat by Grandmother's side, his gaze fixed at her—the almost-still figure in the bed—with his back supported against the wall. Grandmother's eyes were closed and her face glistened in the light of the oil lamp. She was barely breathing. Nilimarani took her mother's hands in hers; they were terribly cold. She held them between her palms and rubbed them, trying to keep them warm.

Grandfather slipped his hand under Grandmother's top, to touch her chest, just below her left breast. She made a small choking sound. He moved his hand and pressed it harder, holding it there for a few minutes. Then, he slumped on his knees beside the bed, as if praying, with his forehead resting at his wife's side and his hand still on her chest.

Nilimarani realized he was crying. It was the most frightening thing that could have happened to her. She lifted her father's face with her hands, tears rolling down his eyes and his lips quivering. 'She is gone,' he said, faintly. She fell over her father's back. She knew it was all over. Her younger sister rushed to the living room to wake up the vaidya, who was sleeping there. He had stayed back in order make himself available in case of an emergency. She rushed back into the room with the vaidya on her heels. He held her mother's wrist and felt her pulse. After a few seconds, he let go of the wrist and it fell on the bed and lay there motionless. 'I'm sorry!' he said, solemnly, making his way out of the room.

Grandfather's cries grew louder. Nilimarani couldn't restrain herself and started wailing too. It was as if her world had come crashing down. Her mother was her biggest support. And now, she was gone. Who would fight for her? Who would be there for her? She knew she had to be strong—for her father and her siblings. She stood up, wiped her tears, gathered herself and went to her father. She assured him that she would always be there by his side.

Grandfather stood up, his gaze still fixed on Grandmother's motionless body. His face was drenched with tears and his hands folded as a gesture of bidding her final goodbye. 'May your soul rest in peace,' he mumbled. He pulled his daughters closer and hugged them. 'Your mother has gone to be with angels, she herself was one,' he whispered. 'Pray for her soul. May she rest in peace.'

Nilimarani wiped her tears and looked at her father, her heart heavy. Everybody stood still, as if struck by a bolt of lightning. Fearing she will break down in front of her father, Nilimarani ran out to the courtyard. It had rained the previous night and the air was still damp and cold. She gazed at the sky, then at the tall coconut and areca nut trees that swayed in the wind. When she was younger, she loved looking at the rhythmic swaying of those tall trees, but now, they meant nothing, they failed to move her.

After the death of Nilimarani's mother, the whole house plummeted into a deafening silence, the place felt like a graveyard. The family members stopped speaking to each other and went about their work silently. Their hearts wailed in silence. Their minds were numb and eyes, tired. There was a void. An overwhelming shroud of emptiness prevailed over the household. It was as if life had come to a tormenting pause, to a complete standstill.

The news of Grandmother's death spread like wildfire. The neighbours came rushing when they heard the wails. As time passed, more and more people started pouring in to pay their last respects and offer their prayers and condolences. Is this a dream? Is this really happening? My mother wondered.

My mother continued to stay at her parental home, taking charge of her two-year-old brother. My mother pulled herself together and somehow continued to care for the family. The death of her mother was a big blow early in her life. The heart-rending experience of losing the person she was most attached to, made my mother stronger and more resilient.

'What is it?' Anadi's words brought Nilimarani back to the present. By now, tears were rolling down her cheeks. Anadi put his hand on her shoulder. Her heart skipped a beat and she felt a tingle. Still caught in her emotions, she dabbed her eyes with her saree.

When they disembarked from the train, Nilimarani was amazed to see so many people on the platform. She had never seen such a rush. Life in the village was easy and slow. My father extended his hand. My mother grabbed it and alighted from the coach. She felt a current run down her spine at that touch. Looking at him, she realized he felt it too. Her rosy cheeks turned even rosier and her breathing grew a little swifter. She pulled down her veil to cover her face completely.

'You don't need a veil here. This is a city, not a village. No one really cares about what the others are doing. They are all busy listening to their own life's music. This is a modern city and progressive thought is the essence of modernity,' he counselled her. But the cultural gap was really big; the new place was centuries ahead than the village in terms of progress. She knew it would be daunting to change and get used to this new way of life, but resolved never to embarrass her husband.

They took a cab home from the railway station. This was the first time she was travelling in a car. They were seated in the back seat of the cab with a mile of space between them. The sights and sounds of the town mesmerized her. She twirled a finger around a lock of her dark hair and shifted uncomfortably in her seat. There was novelty about everything that her eyes met through the cab's window.

'Mrs Samanta, here we are!' Anadi said as the cab pulled up in front of their quarter. They unloaded their luggage and made their way to their new home. 'Step in and relax,' said Anadi, ushering his wife in. 'It's more comfortable here than in the village. There are no oil lamps, lights glow with electricity; to dry sweat off your body, you have a ceiling fan; there is tap water, you don't need to fetch water in pitchers from the river; there is a stove, you don't have to go out to collect firewood. You don't have to walk on mud floors, these are cement floors. Look how smooth they are! There are big markets and you can buy all you need—grocery, vegetable, fish, meat...' he said proudly.

The quarter had two unauthorized add-on rooms, a courtyard, a latrine and a washroom. There was a narrow front porch and a small porch leading to the courtyard. There were four cupboards in the room for storage. Anadi had enclosed a portion of the frontage with a green fence and a wooden gate. While the countryside offered a quiet, scenic backdrop, it lacked many of the advantages that living in the town entailed.

Looking around the house, Nilimarani finally said, 'Amazing, indeed!' She surveyed the house from one end to the other as she walked gracefully around it. After taking a tour of her new home, she returned to the main room, cast a very sweetish smile and said, 'Oh, what a mess you have made, Mr Anadi Samanta! Come, help me clean it.' She hadn't spoken much to him all through the journey and was lost in her thoughts, so these words came as a welcome relief.

Nilimarani busied herself with cleaning the house. Anadi helped her. Soon the house looked livable. She converted what was once a bachelor's den to a home. Anadi demonstrated to her how to make a fire in the coal stove. They prepared their first meal together. If he is always so warm and grounded, my life will be blissful, Nilimarani reflected.

By the time they had their lunch, it was already late in the afternoon. Both were very tired from the journey and cleaning the house. They needed some rest. Anadi took out a bedroll and tried spreading it out on the floor over a reed mattress. But Nilimarani stopped him, 'Leave that to me please. You will not take a step more! Just tell me what you want done and I will do it!'

'Let you do it? I protest. You must excuse me, but I have always taken care of these things at home.' Anadi sounded assertive and dominating, but Nilimarani didn't budge. Anadi was left with no choice but to smile and relent.

When the bed was made, he placed a pillow on it and asked her to lie down. But she hesitated, for there was only one bed. Anadi understood the reason for her hesitation and took out another mattress and laid it on the floor, a little away from hers.

She pleaded with Anadi to sleep on the bed that she had made for him. 'You will offend my address as your wife if you don't listen to my command, sir. It is you who needs to rest as you will be working at the plant tomorrow.'

Both were too tired to argue any further and dozed off without any further ado. Anadi slept on the cotton mattress, while Nilimarani on the reed one.

They were woken up by a knock on the door. It was the woman from next door, 'It is indeed very uncaring of you not to inform us about your bride's coming to stay with you, Mr Samanta,' she accused playfully.

'It's great to have you here Mrs...' The lady went to Nilimarani, but she was interrupted by Anadi.

'She is Nilimarani,' Anadi said. 'Well, I was thinking of calling you. I am on my way to the market now. In the meanwhile, you both can converse, madam.'

The woman spoke to her in Hindi. Nilimarani initially had trouble understanding what the woman was saying, but she put two and two together. She was excited to have a new friend in town. Later in the afternoon, a few more women from the neighbourhood, too, came to welcome their new neighbour. They were mostly from Bengal and Bihar. Nilimarani now had a group of multilingual friends. She herself spoke two languages—Odia and Bengali, so she had no problem communicating with them.

Anadi and Nilimarani visited the nearby vegetable market the following Sunday. Anadi rode to the market on his bicycle with Nilimarani seated on the pillion seat. The market was bustling with activity—buyers buying and haggling and sellers selling. For Nilimarani, it was her first experience of being at a town market. Back in the village, they had no such market. She had, of course, heard from her father that there was a Sunday market. By the time they returned home, it was noon.

Another Sunday, Anadi took her to the nearest cinema hall.

On weekends, the movie hall was very crowded. Anadi wanted Nilimarani to get over the sadness of her mother's demise. Moreover, he thought she might be feeling lonely at home. The movie was a good deviation from the routine household chores. She had difficulty comprehending the dialogues initially, nevertheless, she enjoyed the movie and it thrilled her; in fact she was so thrilled that she insisted on coming for a movie every weekend. The intriguing plot, the moving black-and-white images on the screen, the lilting music, the songs and dances, the sensual scenes—everything was overwhelming for her.

The regular outings, the socializing with neighbours and the weekly trips to the market broke the ice between Nilimarani and Anadi, and they began to communicate more freely. Nilimarani's personality helped her socialize with her neighbours. She became the centre of attraction in the neighbourhood, although she didn't crave the spotlight. She credited her parents for teaching her good manners and how to talk to people. Her sense of humour and wit made it almost impossible for anyone to keep a straight face. 'There are situations in life where it's very difficult to not lose it completely, especially, if something goes wrong. You have to laugh at yourself because if you can't, you may as well give up,' she would often tell her friends. Under the velvety charms and cooing voice hid a steely resolve.

Anadi had a 10 a.m.–6 p.m. shift. His leisure time was spent gossiping with friends and colleagues. They would often drop by at their home, as they got along well with Nilimarani, too.

Relocating to Jamshedpur was a major event in Nilimarani's life. Though she was new there, her neighbours made her feel at home. Everyone was extremely helpful, giving her tips and guiding her through her home-making journey. She received the love and support of her husband and she had begun to admire him. Staying true to their marriage vows, they became each other's friend and love.

Nilimarani was a late riser. But once up, she never rested and handled the household chores well. Sometimes she found the chores overwhelming and monotonous, but she always kept at it. Gardening was one of her passions. Luckily, there was a small frontage which she converted into a small garden. She'd be out in her garden during her free time.

When Anadi took his bicycle out to leave home for work, she would rush to the door and say 'ride safe and come back soon!' She would then linger on at the threshold till her husband was out of sight. She would bask in the sun and enjoy the morning breeze. She felt bubbly and happy when the morning sunlight enveloped her.

When it was time for Anadi to return home, she would wait eagerly by the window, her face pressed against the railing and her eyes glued to the road through which he came. This waiting in anticipation of his arrival gave her a strange pleasure. On his return, he would make a lot of fuss: 'Nilima, give me this,' 'Nilima, give me that' and she would happily oblige.

To be married means having faith and unconditional trust in each other. People get into a marriage because they have faith in this institution and feel safe and secure in a committed relationship. They accept each other's past and look forward to a future together. As for Anadi, although he was still a stranger to his wife, her happiness and well-being were paramount to him.

Like most other young women, Nilimarani began her married life with the determination to be a model housekeeper. He should find our home to be like a paradise; he should always see a smiling face; he should come home to a sumptuous meal; she should never find a button of his shirt or trousers missing, she always told herself. Although she went about her work with a cheerful and positive attitude, there were obstacles. At times, she would try too hard to please her husband, leaving her anxious and stressed out. Sometimes, she was too tired to smile. She loved cooking and feeding her husband. She prepared dishes which were rich and tasty, and Anadi would sometimes become dyspeptic and demand with a smile that she make bland dishes instead—water-soaked rice with lots of greens fry. As for the buttons, they did go missing once in a while and she would accuse Anadi of being careless and jokingly threaten to make him sew them himself.

Nilimarani was very fond of pithas and was quite good at making a variety of them. Every weekend was pancake time. With a practiced hand, she would ladle the creamy batter on to the sizzling circular griddle. Standing at the kitchen door with a smile of admiration, Anadi, would watch her swirl the mixture evenly into a thin round circle and then flip it over with a spatula. Nilimarani would sneak a glance at her husband and smile too and the smile would light up her face.

Since she was so fond of cooking, she learnt new recipes from her neighbours too. She would make pithas and share them with her neighbour. She even taught her how to make the delicious Odia pitha. Nilimarani always made sure that the kitchen was well-stocked. She requested Anadi to buy a few pots so that she could store home-made sweetmeats in them. These items were ideal for breakfast and as packed lunches. She also made mango pickle.

One night, when both the husband and wife were conversing, Anadi said, 'You are the mistress of this household. I will give you everything.'

'Yes, dear husband, have you ever thought of how beautiful our relationship is? I wonder if we could have had such freedom in the village. We are so open to each other and have nothing to hide. No veil, no fear but only love and respect for each other, accepting each other unconditionally!'

They trusted and respected each other and a beautiful friendship bloomed between them. They started sharing each other's secrets and being their real selves in each other's company. Anadi found in her many admirable qualities. She was an infinite source of love, care, trust, respect and understanding. She is my universe now, he would say to himself.

She wished her mother was alive to see her so happy and settled in her married life. She missed her mother every day.

Anadi was an affable person and loved to indulge in feasting with his friends. Nilimarani often said, 'My husband should always feel comfortable bringing a friend home. I will be prepared. There will be no hesitation from my end. They will come to a neat house, a cheerful host and great food. My dear husband, you don't have to ask for my permission, invite whoever you please, and be sure of a warm welcome.'

That was quite enterprising of her. Anadi glowed with pride when he heard her say that and he knew he was blessed to have a wife who felt that way. They had company from time to time and Nilimarani played the welcoming and warm host. They mostly had people visiting from their village on special occasions and festivals. Anadi felt happy and proud of his wife's culinary skills and the way she hosted the gatherings. Sometimes, he brought home a friend or colleague without prior notice, and although she could only prepare a simple meal on such short notice, her warm smile and hospitality more than made up for it.

Anadi was a vegetarian, but he got fish for his wife twice a week. Anadi treated her like a princess and these gestures made her feel special. She had to simply mention it to him and he would take her out to the cinema hall on weekends or to the park.

The city buzzed with activities right from daybreak to late evening. The nights were usually quiet except for the company's siren tearing through the silence and nudging the men on duty to get ready for work. Nilimarani was overwhelmed by so many people from diverse communities and from so many different places. She wanted to explore more. Time seemed to pass by. She was never as happy with anyone as she was with Anadi. Her heart swayed to the beat of his heart.

Autumn set in and a mild breeze begin to blow. The slight nip in the air and the fallen crimson leaves reminded Nilimarani of Dussehra. She wondered if she could go back to the village to be a part of the Durga Puja festival. The very thought of the village made her nostalgic. She waited all day for Anadi to return so she could speak her mind.

One Sunday, Anadi and Nilimarani went to Jubilee Park, a sprawling park with fountains, rose gardens, lush green lawns and beautiful pruned trees. It was a usual hang-out for couples who went there to relax and be by themselves, in the midst of nature. There was a big lake at one end of the park and a well-furnished restaurant by that lake. The restaurant had floor-to-ceiling glass windows which offered a beautiful view of the 100-meter-high fountain at the centre of the lake.

They loitered around the park, enjoying the calm, serene beauty of the autumn afternoon. 'Oh, how delightful! The silence here is like in a prayer room, isn't it?' said Nilimarani, looking at the bright sky. 'How I love this greenery, this pristine beauty of nature. It is so comforting to creep away now and then and come here for a walk among the plants and the flowers and the gurgling fountains. I feel so happy here. This little spot is a dream, a piece of heaven on earth. This place is indeed very dear to me. If I am ever sad, you will find me here,' she said dreamily.

'I hope no great sorrow ever befalls you, Nilima,' said Anadi, who could not connect the idea of sorrow with the joyous and cheerful person standing beside him. 'If I had my way, I would shut everything else out of your life but for happiness and pleasure. We mustn't talk of sorrow on an afternoon like this.'

There were marble benches all along the fountain where one could lounge and watch the water change colour. They selected one of the benches and sat down. They talked about their life, his job and their families. They also talked about the difference between life in the village and life in Jamshedpur.

5

NOT ENOUGH PENNIES

Gradually, Nilimarani and Anadi discovered the key to marital happiness—love and mutual respect. By then, both of them knew each other quite well and the time spent together was enough for them to fall in love with each other. He was charming, lively and entertaining. Her presence in his life made it better. Undaunted by hurdles and hiccups in life, they walked side by side, being each other's friend in the truest sense of the word. Nilimarani realized that a woman's happiest place was at home. To be a wife and to be a mother was the highest honour for her.

Nilimarani was born with extraordinary fate. Although she was born to wealth, at the young age of twenty-one, she found herself submitting to new attachments and relationships and taking on new duties. Anadi found the happiness that he deserved. In Nilimarani, he found a true companion. They were committed and devoted to each other. She stood tall like a coconut palm tree, her strength and her beauty amazed him. In search of the radiant sunlight, they braved every storm, together, and learned much from each other in the process.

One weekend, Anadi was still in bed, lazing around. Nilimarani was drying her hair in the courtyard after a bath when the sky grew darker and it began to rain. The breeze caressed her face and she looked up at the sky. The pitter-patter of the raindrops grabbed her attention. Is the sound of rain always this pleasant? she wondered. She sat at the threshold of the front porch. Outside, the trees were swaying like drunken men. The spray of the drizzle hit her face. She extended her cupped palms outwards to gather the falling droplets. The rain reminded her of her childhood days in the village. During the day, they would go out hunting for the red velvet mites that came out after a shower. At night, they would listen to the cacophony of the sound made by frogs and crickets. Her heart throbbed every time the memories of her childhood crept into her heart, which was often. She inhaled the fragrance of the moist earth, trying to relive the memories of childhood.

She was awakened from her reverie by a baby's cry. It was their first child, a girl. She was born in 1951. They named her Nirupama. The arrival of the baby was the beginning of a new life for them. When Anadi heard the baby cry, he said, 'Nilima, I can't describe how proud I am of you, my brave and beautiful wife. I promise to be the best father to our daughter. I will protect and keep you and our daughter safe to the best of my abilities.'

Their life wasn't the same again. Nothing could have brought more joy and pride to the family than the birth of their first child. They were overcome with joy as they held the baby in their arms. With the arrival of the child, their old life was replaced with a new one. She sought and received the much-needed help from her neighbours, especially the women. She became more loving and patient. Instead of being angry or irritated when the baby cried inconsolably at the dead of night, she nursed it back to sleep. Every time she looked at the baby, her heart skipped a beat. As she watched her baby sleep, she hoped and prayed that she would be able to do everything right. She promised to do her best every single day. What will she be when she grows up? she would often wonder. The baby was Anadi's little angel. Being a mother herself, Nilimarani developed newfound respect for all parents and realized how challenging a job it was. Any other parents' tragedy or triumph struck a chord in her. When the news of the baby's arrival reached their families in the village, they were overjoyed and they performed a number of rituals and ceremonies.

Motherhood was surely one of life's most rewarding experiences, but it was not without its fair share of challenges. The first twelve months after the baby's birth were surreal. Sleepless nights, being on their toes all the time... Every day she woke up with a dizzy dream about the happy times they shared together, which she treasured. She was not prepared for the realities of motherhood. The first few months saw them receiving many visitors, who came to shower their blessings. Her life centered around the baby. Waking up as early as four in the morning and taking care of the baby the whole day was daunting at times.

'What sort of a father are you? You don't even know how to calm her down. How am I supposed to look after the kid and do the household chores if you won't help me? It is *our* child. You have to take equal responsibility,' Nilimarani said curtly one day, chopping onions.

He was browsing the morning newspaper. He loved kids but had no clue how to babysit. He feared his incompetence might hurt the child. Nilimarani watched the scene with amusement, at his awkwardness, as he tended to the baby with utmost care and tried to soothe her. When she saw the baby's father fumble, she dropped her work, washed her hands and walked towards the baby. She scooped up the wailing baby, planted her on her hips and nursed her. The baby became quiet at once. Nilimarani had her first realization of the pride of being a mother.

Motherhood made Nilimarani very efficient. She started to realize the value of twenty minutes in a day. The house looked a little messy though. With the new addition to the family, her priorities changed.

As they watched the little baby sleep, Anadi looked at it lovingly.

Who would have thought that such a beautiful angel will be ours? The baby drew tiny breaths in rapid succession. The baby's fiery red lips curved in a faint smile, as if reading her father's thoughts.

The baby touched Nilimarani's soul; she was the missing link that made her life whole. The mother's heart jumped with joy on seeing those beautiful tiny glittering eyes stare at her. What does she dream of? Nilimarani wondered out loud. Anadi shrugged and smiled warmly at his wife.

Anadi's heart was filled with gratitude too. As time passed by, he grew all the more grateful for every minute he spent with his baby girl. 'Our parents will be as smitten with our daughter as we are,' he quipped. He wished his parents were by his side to experience this beautiful moment.

'Our daughter is precious,' remarked Nilimarani.

'Yes, our daughter is indeed precious,' said Anadi as he continued to watch the baby. A spell of a luminescent smile adorned Nilimarani's lips.

Nilimarani. One word! Eleven letters! Nilimarani, Anadi thought, is a woman with grace and generosity, whose love and devotion to the family redefined my life. She redefined what a home meant to Anadi. She brought him happiness that was no less than divine and contentment that he had never known before. Now, with her and their child, their family was complete. Anadi had everything he had ever dreamed of. He felt like his heart would burst with joy. The baby kept all his restlessness at bay. She was an extension of him. When he held his baby in his arms, all self-doubts disappeared. The house exuded warmth and love. No roaring wind, no tides could crush their faith in each other, and with the baby around, they would never be lonely. With Nilimarani and their daughter, Anadi found a new purpose in life.

As for Nilimarani, she could ask for nothing more and would ask for nothing more, because she realized that her life was with her husband and their child. 'Time decides our fate, our journey and when time changes, everything changes with it. Sometimes for the worse, sometimes for the best,' she realized during the course of her life's journey.

One day, Anandi and Neeliamrani were studying their beautiful girl. Anadi was resting beside the baby, cradling her. The baby had wispy, dark hair, pearl-like eyes—like her mother, chubby cheeks and heart-shaped lips pursed in an adorable pout. Nilimarani held her daughter's fingers and exclaimed, 'She is perfect, isn't she?

'Yes, dear Nilima, she is perfect.'

A year passed and Nilimarani gave birth to a baby boy, Antaryami (Mantoo). When their daughter was only three months old, she found out that she was expecting her second child. The pregnancy wasn't planned and it made her upset. Nilimarani was worried about the short age gap between the two children. Anadi fetched his mother soon after the birth of the first child to help his wife out during her unexpected pregnancy. The apprehension was, however, only short-lived. The couple felt very lucky when they were blessed with a healthy baby boy.

'How is my little boy?' Anadi exclaimed in a loud whisper, holding his firstborn on his lap. He was by Nilimarani's bed after she came out of the labour room to the ward.

'With its mother.'

'How are you feeling?'

'Happy as a queen.' Nilimarani's face was very sober, but her eyes twinkled and her voice was laced with emotion.

Anadi put their firstborn by her side and held out his hands to hold the new baby. His happiness knew no bounds when he held his son for the first time.

When they returned from the hospital, Anadi's mother suggested that she take her granddaughter with her to the village so that Nilimarani would be able to look after the newborn better. After a lot of soul-searching, they finally agreed to send their daughter off to the village with her grandmother.

Over the course of time, the couple was blessed with five more children—Anupama, Annirudhha, Achyuta, Trupti and Iti. Anadi saw his loving wife go through very long labour every time she gave birth. He felt sorry for her and did feel guilty. But she made the choice of having the children because she knew that she would be able to go through their births, as she had never wished ill for anyone. She meant what she said. That was Nilimarani for you! Her simplicity was inspiring and even in trying times, she tried to keep her head above the water.

Although each new addition to the family brought immense happiness, the big family took a toll on the expenses. The couple often had squabbles. 'Take care of the pennies and the pounds will take care of themselves' she had one day admonished him, referring to his increasing expenses on court cases. He was pursuing a legal battle against his paternal uncle at that time and also buying souvenirs for fellow villagers every time he went to the village.

One evening, Anadi came home with a friend for dinner. At first he hesitated before softly rapping on the door. When the door was opened by one of his children, he asked his friend to wait in the living room and nervously informed Nilimarani, who was in the kitchen, that he had brought home a friend for dinner. He had also bought a big fish. He knew Nilimarani was crazy about fish. They were hungry, too. They had come straight from work, picking up the fish on their way. What ensued thereafter was a very upsetting conversation between the two.

'What!? Someone for dinner, when I'm neck deep in a mess, looking after the kids, with very little money. And if that's not enough, you bring home a fish to be cooked at this hour. Dear Mr Samanta, how could you do such a thing? How could you be so heartless? Where did your good senses go, grazing in the moor?'

'Shhh... He's in the room! I am sorry about that, but it can't be helped now,' said Anadi, surveying her with an anxious eye.

'You ought to have sent a word or told me this morning, and you ought to have remembered how busy I stay with the household chores, and on top of that, the children and their ever-increasing tantrums!' continued Nilimarani petulantly, for even turtledoves peck when ruffled.

'I didn't know this morning, and there was no time to send word, for I met him on the way out. I didn't think asking you was necessary, as I have always known that you love having guests over.'

'Take him away at once. I can't see him, and there isn't any dinner. I don't have the time to cook now. I thought you will lend me a helping hand once you come home. It has been a very long day for me.'

Anadi was a mild man, sober and sympathetic. But he was human too. After a long day at work, tired and hungry, the last thing he wanted was a chaotic house and an angry wife. But he kept his calm.

'It's a scrape, I acknowledge, but if you will lend me a hand, we'll pull this through and have a good time. Don't yell, dear. Just relax and fix something to eat. We're both famished, and we shan't mind whatever it is you serve.'

'You must get yourself out of the scrape as you can. I won't have anything of that sort in my house anymore. Just take him out for dinner. I can't do anything now,' she delivered all her defiance in one breathe. What followed was a sharp exchange of words.

'Everything's so useless...being in love, quarreling, making up...'

'Mantoo's father, you expect so much from me, it's suffocating.'

'Well, I do. I want us to be everything to each other.'

'But that's so suffocating.'

'God, God, God.'

A thick cloud of dismay and despair took over both. The future seemed grim. Both, however, did not like quarrelling in front of the children and in the presence of the guest. They were wrong in believing that life will be easy. The years had passed by in the blink of an eye. The moments of joy had flown by. Life wasn't easy and struggles crept into their life. The painting of love which both Nilimarani and Anadi had created was beginning to fade. She wanted to cry aloud, but couldn't.

She got dressed and began to cook while he lent her a helping hand as his friend played with the children.

When the friend was gone, Anadi softly expressed his disappointment, 'It wasn't fair to tell me to bring friends home at any time, when you are yourself flared up and leaving me in a lurch. When you said that I am always free to get my friends home, I took your word for it.'

She didn't answer but just stared at him submissively. She then rose from where she was sitting, walked across the courtyard and opened the door. She stretched her arms as much as she could. She let out a sigh, turning her face towards the crisp and gentle breeze; it cooled her down. Then, she came into the house, closing the door behind her. The gush of wind whistled through a crack in the sapling panels of the door as she walked back heavily to the verandah. Anadi turned to look at Nilimarani with wide eyes. She stared at him with a blank expression and raised her eyebrows in a manner that suggested that she expected an explanation.

Anadi softened, 'Poor thing! I shouldn't have done it. It must surely be hard on her. She is trying so much to please me. She was wrong, of course, but then I was insensible too. I should be patient with her.' The thought softened him and he resolved to be calm and kind.

Nilimarani, likewise, resolved to be calm and kind too. 'Anadi is a good man, but he has his faults too, like any other human being. I must learn to discern and bear with them, remembering my own limitations. He is very determined, but will never be obstinate if I reason gently. He is very particular about the truth, which is a good trait. He gave me the confidence I lacked and the support I needed.' Nilimarani reasoned with herself. So she never hesitated to apologize when she was wrong.

The next evening, she sat sewing. Her thoughts kept going back to the previous evening's unpleasant proceedings with her husband. This was their first serious disagreement, both had sounded silly and unkind. Looking back, her own anger looked so childish, and the thoughts of poor Anadi melted her heart. That evening, Anadi came home earlier than usual. When he entered the room, she glanced at him with tears in her eyes; she put aside what she was doing and got up. Very slowly, she went across the room and stood by him as he parked his bicycle in the courtyard and whispered, 'I am sorry for yesterday. Forgive me.'

That was one of many fights the couple had about finances. The constraint of money troubled Nilimarani. Both then avoided crossing each other's path and maintained discreteness, careful about the adverse impact their squabbles would have on the kids.

For the next few years, Anadi was barely home before midnight. He went off to work early in the morning, skipping breakfast. His near-absence from home pricked both Nilimarani and the children. One day, as Anadi was getting ready to go out, she accosted him, 'Don't go now, don't go now, Mantoo's father! You haven't even had your breakfast.' She pleaded again, 'This is not fair. You're killing yourself. Please don't. The children miss your presence around the house.'

Nilimarani knew he was being unreasonable. Maybe he needs a nudge and that is what I will do, she resolved. He didn't reply. Both fell silent for a few seconds.

When she noticed that Anadi did not soften, she clasped his wrists and gave him a judder, 'Your forebears will be turning in their graves.' Her eyes were red. She opened her mouth to speak, but found herself at a loss for words. Ultimately, she let go of his wrist, without uttering a single word.

He was gone.

Nilimarani was taking a nap when she was suddenly awakened by repeated knocks on the door. It was evening. She looked out of the window. There he was—Anadi, holding something in his hand. She rushed to the door and opened it. He was in front of her, smiling. He handed over a parcel. 'For the kids,' he said. She felt happy. Anadi was back in her life.

They hadn't had a lavish feast in a long time owing to the financial crunch. She had gradually stopped socializing with her neighbours. With seven children around the house, she couldn't ask her friends from the neighbourhood to come over and even if they did, she wasn't willing to commit unnecessary expenses. This left her feeling lonely. Very soon, the older children got busy with their studies, and Anadi, as usual, was away from home till late into the evening. Although she was so fond of cooking and trying out new recipes, her culinary journey had stopped long back. Looking after the kids and the home left her too tired to do anything else.

Nilimarani knew how much her husband's income was. She felt her husband trusted her when she was made privy to that information. She knew where he kept his money and was free to take what she needed. All he expected of his wife was to keep tab of the accounts and be frugal with money—not that she was not frugal herself. In fact, it was she who reminded him to be careful with his expenses and she always maintained an account book. At the end of the month, they would go through the notebook and evaluate their expenses. She was not parsimonious either.

Everything was going well until this 'serpent' got into her paradise. They couldn't even afford to buy a full month's grocery. She had to curtail daily household expenses to save for Dussehra, so that she could buy new dresses for the children. Even then, it didn't suffice. She rarely visited the market with her neighbours fearing that her financial constraint would be noticed. They stopped gadding about in town—something they did whenever they had free time.

The situation eventually forced Anadi to secretly fall upon borrowing from his colleagues. Nilimarani noticed that, as she always kept a check on the household fund. It pained her that he didn't confide in her about it, but she didn't say anything, fearing another row.

However, one day, she couldn't hold herself back. 'You haven't seen our house-fund account this month yet?' she accosted Anadi.

Anadi knew that she was vehemently against borrowing and for many months, he hadn't checked the accounts book. She insisted that he take a look at the book. She wanted him to evaluate his spending pattern so that they could find out the reason for their depleting finances. The little book was brought out and laid in front of him. She looked away under the pretense of fixing her hair. Anadi refused to look at it. He knew she wanted to prove him guilty. Finally the cat was out of the bag. 'Look, Mantoo's father, you should be ashamed of borrowing from your friends.'

'Oh, don't worry; I will pay it back when I get the bonus,' he promised.

'I know you are angry, Mantoo's father, but I can't help it. I can't digest the idea of living on borrowed money. I prefer to starve than live on borrowed money. We are not able to meet the month's expenses, with the family increasing in number. Maybe we can have some side business, home-based, to stave off financial stringency, at least to some extent.'

The last words were spoken so softly that she thought he hadn't heard them, but he had, and they hurt him deeply. He was already denying himself many pleasures for the sake of his family. She could see the dismay on his face. I should have bitten my tongue, she thought to herself. Anadi pushed the account book away and got up. 'I was afraid it would come to this. I am doing my best, Nilima. I couldn't see you all starve like that. I don't borrow for *my* comfortable living. I know that you don't need much for yourself. But it is our children who need our support the most. I am doing it for them,' he said, his voice quivering.

That day, Anadi went on quietly afterward, just as if nothing had happened, except that he worked extra hours. Nilimarani was fraught with worry. That night, Anadi and Nilimarani had a long talk. With time, she learned to love her husband better—with or without the comfort that money brought. She gave him the strength and courage to fight this battle, taught him how to patiently deal with these challenges. Of all the people in her life, she loved and cared for him the most. Yet another lesson learnt—resolve issues through amicable talks!

The next day, she swallowed her pride and went over to her neighbour to talk about their financial condition. After a long conversation and brainstorming, they decided to start making cow-dung pellets and cow-dung cakes, which they would sell in the neighbourhood, to be used as fuel, especially for cooking. She started making the preparations after consulting her eldest son, Mantoo and second daughter, Trupti, who agreed to assist her in the business by collecting cow dung. Cows and buffaloes strolled around freely in the streets and it wasn't difficult to collect cow dung. The business picked momentum over time and soon, the income was decent enough to meet a good part of their household expenses. She had by then brutally slashed all avoidable expenses and minimized their needs. She explained to the children the reason for the curtailing of their expenses. She roped in all the resources at her disposal to expand the volume of her business, so that Anadi's salary could be used exclusively for repaying the debts.

During that time, Anadi had to make frequent visits to the village and Cuttack to pursue the legal battle around his share of the ancestral property. Legal battles are expensive affairs and continue for many years, and theirs was no exception. The court fees, the advocate's charges and other miscellaneous expenses of the court were a drain on his salary. That apart, the children's expenses, the household expenses, the payment of interest on loans and sending money to his parents made a big dent in his pocket. Financial crunch was crushing him. Hesitatingly, he resorted to borrowing from kabuliwallas (Afghan money lenders). He was up to his neck in debt. Nilimarani got a hint about him borrowing money, but she dared not accost him again.

Autumn was setting in and that meant additional expenses for Dussehra. One day, a harried Nilimarani sat with her eldest son, Mantoo, who was in Class XI then, at the doorstep, discussing their business and finances. As they sat talking, Nilimarani caught sight of the newspaper hawker who had once delivered the Odia newspaper, *The Samaj*, at their house. It was Anadi's favourite newspaper. She waved at the hawker, gesturing him to come in. She inquired if Mantoo could join him in delivering newspapers. He replied in the affirmative. The challenge was that Mantoo would need a bicycle for that and his boards were approaching. The bright side was that he had a couple of hours to spare in the morning. Later in the evening, when Anadi returned home, she pleaded with him to buy Mantoo a bicycle. Soon a bicycle was bought and Mantoo started delivering newspapers in the neighbourhood.

One day, when one of Mantoo's friends saw him delivering newspapers, he felt embarrassed. 'I will not continue with this work. My friends laugh at me.' He narrated the whole incident to his mother.

'It's okay if you don't want to continue, son, but remember one thing, no job is insignificant.'

6

THUNDER STRIKES

One day, Nilimarani was awakened by the loud blaring of the company siren. She checked the time on the wall clock. It was midnight. The midnight sirens are usually longer, she thought to herself. The children had had their dinner and were fast asleep.

The only window in the room was open, allowing a cool breeze to drift in. The moon was up in the sky. A ray of moonlight sneaked into the room through the open window. Suddenly, the room became dark as clouds hid the moon.

Nilimarani sat up in her bed. Stretching her neck, she looked around the room. Her children were fast asleep. As she surveyed the room, she felt a strange vibration pulsating inside her. She lay down, closed her eyes and tried to catch some sleep.

A good night's sleep was what she needed at the end of the day's drudgery. Good sleep would let her get over the meaningless gossamer of dreams that kept her awake at nights. Exhausted, she fell asleep, but woke up suddenly, startled. Another nightmare, she sighed. She sat up with her legs folded and drawn in towards her. Resting her chin on her knees, she began ruminating over the dream. She rubbed her eyes, but they still felt heavy and weary. She lifted her head and let out a big yawn. Once again she swept the room with her sleepy gaze.

Unable to sleep, her thoughts drifted to her past. Twenty-six years. *I have been married for twenty-six years now.* She was blessed with seven beautiful and healthy children. A bigger family meant more expenses and they reeled under the pressure of growing expenditure. She took care of the house and the children when her husband toiled away in the factory. Despite all the hard work that they put in, they were not financially strong. They had to bury all their dreams and aspirations with their bare hands that were now rough and aged from hard work. This was not the life she had envisioned for herself when she married the handsome Anadi Samanta. She grew restless.

The face of her husband flashed in her mind's eye. They were trying very hard to overcome the financial crisis and support the children the best they can. They often fasted so that the children had a few morsels to eat. The growing financial burden created a rift between the couple and they had frequent fights and quarrels. The initial years were smooth. The children were happy. There was no shortage of any kind. The children were studying in some of the best schools. When did things start going downhill? She wondered, looking out of the window to catch a glimpse of the night sky. Ominous lumps of clouds were covering the moon, casting foreboding shadows on the walls. She came back to bed and rested her head on the pillow. She closed her eyes, but her thoughts kept wandering back to the good old times—her happy childhood, her wedding, the time spent with her in-laws and her initial years in Jamshedpur.

She sniffled a little, her eyes were puffy and moist. She battled with her intuitive thoughts. The picture of her husband came to her mind again. She had known him for twenty-six years. He looked older than his age now. There were patches of grey hair on his head. His complexion had started paling; his eyes said he needed sleep. He had grown a stubble, making him look all the more tired and haggard.

She restlessly turned from side to side on her mattress but could not wriggle out of her tormenting thoughts. She got up and leaned her head on the wall behind her, her gaze fixed at the murky ceiling. Her eyes grew heavy, she forced them open. Stretching her upper body, she looked tenderly at her sleeping children. The sight of them sleeping peacefully calmed her frayed nerves. She yearned to hug her siblings.

It was already well past midnight and time was lazily crawling towards dawn. Somewhere a dog barked. She rose and glided quietly from one bed to another, smoothing a coverlet here, settling a pillow under a sleeping head there. She took a moment to look at the peaceful faces, planting a light kiss on their foreheads, careful not to wake them up. She folded her hands and said a silent prayer for the well-being of her children.

Her gaze turned to the open window. Something coaxed her to go there. She sneaked a glance at the dreary night. The moon suddenly came out from behind the clouds and shone before her like a bright benignant face. Enchanted, she kept on looking at the moon, as if she was being lulled into a trance. The benignant face of the moon seemed to whisper to her, 'Be comforted, dear soul! Go and sleep! There is always light behind the clouds.'

Sometimes fate brought in gut-wrenching surprises. Anadi was on his way to Cuttack with my maternal grandfather and my eldest sister, who had come to visit as her school was closed for the holidays. Nilimarani eagerly awaited word from them about their reaching Cuttack. Grandfather was not well; he had broken one of his arms in an accident and she was impatient to know if her father was alright.

Grandfather was not able to visit his daughter when she gave birth to her seventh child. Every time she gave birth to a child, her father visited to bless the new member of the family. He brought along with him fruits and sweetmeats. The children were very fond of their grandfather. He showered them with love and affection and looked for an opportunity to visit Jamshedpur.

This time, he and my eldest sister were in Jamshedpur for a week. Their presence made the household bounce with joy. We were having a great time when our grandfather met with an accident...

It was a Saturday. My father was home that day. The children were gaily romping around the house. The lunch menu for that day was enticing. The fish curry was the best and the children and Nilimarani enjoyed it the most.

After lunch, my father and grandfather had a quiet conference. After taking a short nap, they headed to the nearest hall, Basant Cinema. They went on my father's cycle. On their way, Father lost his balance and both fell down on the road. Actually, Grandfather tried to shift his position on the pillion seat and the bicycle wobbled. Father lost his grip and it tipped over on to the right side of the road.

When Father reached out to Grandfather to help him up, he was moaning in pain. He was unable to lift his right hand, the pain was excruciating. My father somehow helped him up to his feet. The limb was swollen, too. Consternated, Father took him to the nearby hospital, where the doctor, after an elaborate examination, declared that Grandfather's forearm was broken. The doctor advised immediate setting of the broken bones and plastering over the affected part. After getting that done, they returned home in a cab. It was almost evening by then. After some rest, Grandfather, who was still writhing in pain, said that he intended to return to Cuttack by the night bus and asked my father to help him buy tickets for him and his granddaughter. Grandfather was nervous. He wanted to go to his son in Cuttack to avail further treatment at the Cuttack Medical College, where he was studying medicine.

Father was concerned. How could he allow his ageing father-in-law with a broken arm and his young daughter to travel all by themselves? On the other hand, he had no leaves. Because of his frequent visits to his village and Cuttack, he had exhausted his leaves. His absence from work at this stage would mean a wage cut, which he could ill afford.

He thought it over and despite the deduction of salary, he decided to accompany his father-in-law and daughter to Cuttack. It was planned that he would drop Grandfather at the main bus station in Cuttack and from there, Grandfather would take a rickshaw to his son's house. Father would put my sister on a bus that would drop her off near Kalarabanka. And then he himself would board a Jamshedpur-bound bus. That way, he would not miss a day at work.

Thus they left together for Cuttack. Mantoo went to the bus station to see them off.

They reached Cuttack at 5.30 the following morning. It was a Sunday. The three of them got off at the main bus station at Badambadi in Cuttack. Father was impelled to change his plan. He felt guilty about sending his father-in-law off all by himself to his son's house. He offered to accompany Grandfather and he readily agreed. They took a cycle rickshaw to Ranihat Square, which is a couple of kilometers from the bus stand. Nilimarani's brother stayed in a boarding house near Ranihat Square.

My father dropped Grandfather off at his son's place, had a brief conversation with his brother-in-law and then returned to the main bus station at Badambadi with my sister. My father did not have the heart to let his daughter go on her own and so decided to accompany her to Kalarabanka.

A bus was to leave for Kalarabanka in an hour. They still had about forty-five minutes in hand. They were starving, so they went to a nearby restaurant. When they reached the station, the bus was about to leave and the driver was honking frantically. A street urchin hollered, announcing the bus's departure. The bus was not headed all the way to Kalarabanka, so they had to get off at the main road, from where they walked to the village, which was at a distance of about two miles. There was no other conveyance available.

After settling his daughter in her grandparents' house, where she had been living for a couple of years now, he immediately returned to the main road, covering the entire distance on foot. He was lucky to get a Cuttack-bound bus no sooner had he hit the main road. When he reached the Badambadi bus station, it was already evening and he was utterly exhausted. He ached for some rest. He could have stayed at his brother-in-law's place for the night, but he had to report for duty the next morning. After all, he didn't have enough leaves left in his account. If he didn't report for his duty, it would mean a day's wage cut. He couldn't afford another wage cut.

From here I should travel to Jamshedpur by train. I will have the whole berth to myself and can catch up on my sleep. And I will save some time too, he thought to himself. So, he made up his mind to take the train to Jamshedpur. The train he intended to board was due to leave in two hours. He was starving. There was enough time, so he walked into a nearby restaurant and had a sumptuous meal. He reached the station in time to board the train.

He had to change trains at Kharagpur because the one he boarded at Cuttack went to the Howrah Station in Calcutta (now Kolkata). The route to Tatanagar was a different one. He was lucky enough to have a berth all to himself and he had a good sleep. The train reached at 5.00 in the morning. The passengers began alighting from the train. After all the people deboarded the train, it whistled and made its way to the maintenance yard. But my father was fast asleep.

A tea vendor passed by the bogie hollering 'tea, tea, tea'. Suddenly, his eyes fell on Father. He got into the bogie and woke him up. My father rubbed his eyes and looked out the window to figure out which station he was at. By that time, the train began to pick up a little speed. He grabbed his luggage and rushed out of the door compartment. He was still in his stupor as he tried to get off the slowly moving train. He lost his balance, slipped on the footboard and fell onto the uneven gravelly ground under the carriage through the narrow space between the edge of the platform and the carriage. The people at the platform started shouting, 'A man has fallen into the tracks... Stop the train... Stop the train!' Someone rushed to the station master's room to inform him about the accident. But the train continued to move until it received a signal from the authorities to pull the brakes. By the time the train screeched to a halt, it had covered a few metres and my father's body was thoroughly crushed under the carriage.

The railway authorities extricated him from under the carriage. He had lost his senses by then. He was taken to the first-aid centre at the railway station. He had wounds all over his body and his bones looked like they were crushed. The authorities decided to send him to the nearest government hospital. When they were making preparations to take him to the railway hospital, they found the Tata Company gate pass in his pocket. He was immediately shifted to

Tata Main Hospital, about five kilometers away from the railway station.

Nilimarani woke up suddenly. It was dawn already. The golden rays of the morning sun adorned the sky. 'Daylight will nudge its way into the room and wake up the children,' she whispered, smiling to herself. She did not expect her husband home till late in the evening, as he was supposed to report for duty directly.

When my father didn't reach home the previous evening, my mother concluded that he must have travelled overnight by train and that he would proceed straightaway from the railway station to the company to report at his duty post.

She stretched her arms and legs. She felt very lazy and let out a couple of yawns before bouncing back on her bed again to get some more sleep before the children woke up. 'There is still some time before the children wake up. I didn't have good sleep last night. I think I will grab a couple more winks,' she reasoned. Soon, she fell asleep.

The blazing sun was up in the sky, lighting the eastern horizon. Suddenly she was woken up by a rap on the door. She was confused. *Am I dreaming?* She opened her eyes, still in a state of stupor. Her eyes were red and puffy. *I could use a few more hours of sleep*, she sighed, rubbing her eyes.

She lifted her head and strained her eyes to look at the door. The knocking had stopped. She rested her head again.

Knock! Knock! Knock...

She sat up again, rubbing her eyes.

Knock! Knock! Knock!

How odd! Who could it be at this hour? Is it Mantoo's father? Why did he not go to his duty? If not him, then who could it be this early in the morning?

The knocking continued. She decided not to open the door at once, for security reasons. She walked up to the window with heavy, clumsy steps to see who it was this unreasonably early in the morning. She slowly pulled one panel of the window and sneaked a glance. There were a couple of men at the door. She had never seen them before.

Are these the people my husband owes money to? She was beginning to fret. She knew that her husband had taken loan from many people. How would she face them? What will she say if they asked about her husband? What would happen if the children woke up and heard them demanding payment of interest accrued on the loans? Nilimarani trembled with fear and her heart began to beat faster. She decided not to open the door and stood by the half-open window, but the visitors continued to knock with a growing sense of urgency. She took a deep breath and decided to face the people anyway. She shouted from across the window, 'Hey, who is it? Why are you rapping at the door like this at this hour? Are you looking for anything?'

The men quickly came to the window. She sneaked a glance at them. They were middle-aged gentlemen, they wore a worried look. One of them came closer to the window. 'I am from the Tata Main Hospital,' he said, holding up the hospital gate pass up as proof of his identity. 'Are you the wife of Anadi Samanta?' There was an urgency in his voice.

Hospital? Was there a mishap with my husband? No, that can't be! Nilimarani's head began to spin.

'Y...Yes, I am his wife,' she replied, her face covered with the free end of her saree. Her mind was now muddled in a murky abyss. 'What is this regarding?' she queried.

'I am extremely s...sorry, but we have some b...bad news for you. It ... It is concerning your hus...husband, Anadi Samanta,' he stuttered, trying to find the right words to convey the message.

There was a lump in her throat. 'Why, what has happened to him? Why do you say bad news?' She slid away from the window and leaned against the wall, her hands folded in a prayer and head turned upwards. Nervousness began gripping her and she found it difficult to concentrate. Her thoughts ran in different directions. Her sixth sense told her that something was horribly wrong. She began to tremble and her heart began to pound.

After a few moments passed and the thoughts that fogged her mind began to clear, she pulled herself together. *I must get the details from those men! But I am still in my sleepwear... and what if this whole thing is just a ploy to get me out of the house?* She at once returned to the window. 'Please wait for a second. I want you to speak to my son. Please wait here!'

She ran to where Mantoo was sleeping. He was already awake and looking anxiously at his mother from under his coverlet.

'Mantoo, there are some men at the door. Please speak to them, they are from the hospital. They told me that it was regarding your father. Please talk to them from the window.'

Mantoo got out of his bed and rushed to the window. The two men standing there looked very restless. 'You must be Mr Anadi Samanta's son...err...what's your name?' one of them asked.

'Mantoo. Yes, I am Mr Samanta's son. Please tell me. What happened to my father? Where is he? And who are you...mmmm...I mean...' His voice giving away his apprehension and worry.

One of the strangers replied hesitatingly, 'Err...We are the staff of the Tata Main Hospital. These are our gate passes.' Mantoo collected the gate passes, examined them and matched the photos with their bearers. He was convinced that the men were genuine and that they were not faking their identity.

The visitor continued, 'Your father is seriously injured. He was brought to our hospital senseless. It is reported that he slipped while getting off a running train at the Tatanagar railway station. You must come to the hospital at once. The injuries could...err...could be...err ...and he may not...mmmm... I mean... the doctors are trying their best, of course. We have been directed by the authorities to inform your mother. Someone from the family is needed to be at the hospital at once...in case... I mean...you understand, don't you? He should still be in the emergency ward. Please hurry!'

Mantoo stood at the window, trying to take everything in. His wits deserted him briefly. However, taking a couple of deep breaths, he questioned the visitor further, 'How do you know that it was my father?'

'They found the Tata Company's gate pass in his pocket. A few of his colleagues are already at the hospital. They rushed to the hospital when they got the news. Even they have identified him. You better hurry! The doctor wants to speak to someone from the family.'

Mantoo felt nauseated and light-headed. His limbs were limp. He held onto the window grill, fearing he might lose his balance. Let it not be true, he prayed. He turned around to talk to his mother. There she was—standing right behind him all the while he had been speaking to the strangers. She had heard it all.

'What shall I do now, Mother?' Mantoo asked.

Nilimarani just stood there like a statue, pale and motionless. Her lips twitched nervously.

Mantoo turned to the visitors and said, 'I know the route to the hospital. I will be there at once. Mother can't come. She is extremely distressed by the news. You can go ahead. I will get my bike and follow you this instant.'

Mantoo took out his cycle and stopped at the front door. He turned to look at his mother. She was still standing at the window, motionless. He rode off. He didn't even turn back to wave goodbye to his mother, like he always did. He pedalled so hard that the chain slipped off the front sprocket a couple of times.

Nilimarani was almost on the verge of fainting. Somehow she dragged herself to the door and closed it behind her. Her body was drained of energy. She could barely stand. She faltered back to her bed and slumped on it.

'Fate has been very unkind to him, but he never stopped to ask why. He has worked so hard his whole life,' she whispered to herself.'

The part of the bed where her head rested was drenched in tears. She had fallen asleep, without even knowing it. When she woke up from her troubled slumber, she gathered herself together and sat cross-legged, her back leaning against the wall. Her gaze was fixed at the ceiling. The words 'bad news' kept ringing in her ears. Tears rolled down her cheeks.

Everyday events always seem unremarkable and ordinary. We understand the gravity of such situations only when they become history, a thing of the past.

My father was never a very religious person, but we noticed that he had become a little more particular than usual about his puja routine. He started waking up as early as three in the morning. He would then finish his morning ablutions and perform an elaborate puja in the east corner of the room—very unlike him.

One Sunday, Nilimarani decided to have a word with him. The children were off to play with their friends in the playground behind their house. My father was fixing his cycle. She stomped up to him and prodded him. 'Listen, Mantoo's father, what is with this madness? Why have you become this religious all of a sudden? What do you keep murmuring in the morning? You start your puja at four in the morning! I see that you have started skipping your breakfast and dinner, too. Why all this penance? I need an explanation this very moment.'

He listened to her patiently, then caught hold of her hand, caressing it lovingly. She cooled down after a while. That's the way she was—one moment a raging tempest and the next, still waters. He began to explain the reason behind his puja rituals, still holding her hand...

'A couple of years ago, on a Sunday, I had gone to the Shiva temple near our house. I used to go there sometimes. That day, I happened to meet a baba there. My life has changed after that meeting. I am doing this penance for the well-being of the family. I am simply following his instruction.

'There is a prayer hall inside the temple premises, where people generally assemble for group chanting on special occasions. Leading to the temple is a path that passes by the prayer hall. That day, as I passed the hall, I saw many people going into it. I ignored the hustle-bustle at the prayer hall and headed straight to the main temple.

'When I returned from the temple, I stopped in front of the hall. The hustle-bustle had receded by then. I was curious and sneaked inside. My gaze fell upon a saffron-robed baba, who was seated on a dais, elaborately decorated with flowers. Baba's feet rested on a well-cushioned stool with a whitish coverlet. There were two round pillows on the dais, one on each side, on which he rested his arms. The entire sanctum sanctorum was beautifully decorated with flowers. A copper kamandalam, water pot, was placed on a stool near Baba.

'The baba, too, was bedecked in several garlands of Araka beads and hibiscus flowers. His forehead was smeared with ash and a thick vermilion mark stretched from the centre of his eyebrows to his grey hairline. His long, grey beard almost touched his navel. Baba's eyes were closed; his face, serene. He seemed to radiate a halo around him.

'A small crowd had assembled in front of Baba; they were seated on the carpeted floor with their legs crossed and their eyes closed. A divine tranquility prevailed inside the hall. The scene looked out of this world. A sweet fragrance enveloped the air inside the hall. My gaze was fixated on the baba. I couldn't take my eyes off him. Baba's serene countenance mesmerized me.

'Although I have been to the temple a number of times, I had never seen any baba visiting. I found it to be strange. As if in a trance, I took a seat at the end of the hall, in a corner, away from the crowd.

'After almost an hour, Baba opened his eyes. He took a few deep breaths and chanted "Om" while exhaling. I was gazing into Baba's eyes unwaveringly. Baba's gaze too was fixated on me, pulling me closer, as if we have known each other for a very long time.

'I kneeled by the side of Baba's footstool with folded hands. Baba chanted "Om Namah Shivaya". He then hinted me to stretch out my right hand with palms facing upwards. Baba held my palm tightly in his right hand, breathed heavily for several minutes, chanted "Om Namah Shivaya" once again and then with his eyes closed, addressed me: "Vatsa, you are a good soul, but I am sorry you have a very short life span; it's all because of your past karma, a few serious faults you committed in some past life. The planet Ketu is malefic to you.

Under its effect, you have not been getting any rise in your profession and you are neck-deep in debt. You are not at peace. Your wife was born with all the qualities of Goddess Durga, but she is unable to help you because she is daunted by your extremely malefic planetary configuration. Your children are all good; however, it is your youngest son who is destined to be a star. He is the mount of the Goddess Durga. Your wife will be his parasol."

'Baba's discourse left me flabbergasted. I shuddered. We were silent for a while. I felt my palm getting warmer. Baba breathed heavily a few more times, chanted "Om Namah Shivaya" and spoke again with his eyes closed: "Vatsa, don't panic. There is a remedy for your predicament, but it needs complete surrender and unfailing worship of Lord Shiva for eight years. The puja is simple. Commit right here and right now, so that I can tell you the process of worship." I committed myself to doing the puja as instructed.

'Baba's eyes were still closed. He breathed heavily and chanted "Om Namah Shivaya" thrice. "Take this blessing that I am going to give you," he said. Baba raised his hand a little, clenched his fist and placed it on my palm. He chanted "Om Namah Shivaya" and a few other mantras. Baba's voice was heavy and solemn. My body temperature was higher than usual; my heart was beating faster and my palm continued to sizzle. I instinctively glanced at my palm and saw a tiny heap of ash resting there.

'Baba took out a twig of Bel leaves and continued with his instructions: "Take this blessing from Lord Shiva and wrap it securely with Bel leaves. Then, put it in a tiny cylindrical copper shell with some vermilion and seal the cylinder with a pure silver slug. At home, tomorrow early morning, after your ablutions, dip this talisman in milk kept in a new silver bowl, then place the milk-washed talisman on a wooden platform covered with a red cloth and chant 'Om Namah Shivay' 108 times. When you complete chanting, bow before the talisman and offer your prayers for your well-being as well as your family's, ridding them of their past and present sins. Then tie the talisman around your waist with a black thread. You must take off the talisman, wrap it in a piece of red cloth and keep it away from your body when you attend to nature's call. Whenever you have some free time, chant the mantra. Sooner you complete one million times of chanting, the better.

'I touched Baba's feet, collected the ash off his feet and smeared the same on my forehead. This is the reason behind my praying so religiously. I am doing it for us, dear.'

Nilimarani sat reflecting on the past. The words of the strangers who came with the news about her husband's accident kept ringing in her ears. Tears rolled down her cheeks. She was reminded of the previous moonlit night. Her head continued to spin as memories of a lifetime wrestled among themselves to come to the fore. When one window of memory closed, another opened. Her head began to ache. She tried her best to keep a check on her emotions and the wavering thoughts. She choked and her breaths got shorter and shorter. She tried to suppress the sobs with all her might, but failed. She began to moan and soon, her moan turned into a loud wail. The children woke up, looking anxiously at her. Frightened, they, too, started crying.

She took a deep breath and hugged her children, consoling them.

The youngest of the children, Iti, was just three months old. She flapped her arms and legs and rolled her head, perhaps trying to figure out what the commotion was about.

'What happened, Mother? Why do you look so sad?' asked one of the children.

Why am I so sad when I know that nothing bad will happen to him and he will come back home, hale and hearty? Nilimarani clutched the free end of her saree and wrapped it around her chest. *Why am I overcome with sorrow? Why am I imagining things?*

Finally, controlling her emotions, she broke her silence, 'Your father has met with an accident and he has been admitted to a hospital. Mantoo has gone there. Let's hope everything is okay with him.' After a brief pause, she continued, 'Let's hope that he is not seriously injured.

Keep praying for him and keep busy with your chores, children!' One by one they obediently went into the courtyard to brush their teeth and for their morning ablutions.

Is his condition critical? Has something bad befallen him? Mantoo has been gone for so long. When it rains, it pours. So true!

Nilimarani continued to sit in the room waiting impatiently for the return of her son with news of her husband's condition. She was expecting both father and son home at the earliest. The wait is the most difficult part. It brings negative and destructive thoughts. Her husband's face from his younger days flashed in her mind's eyes. His neatly combed thick raven hair, his eyes exuding warmth and fixed on her, and the endearing smile lingering on his lips. *I hope he is fine.*

She could not take it any more. *I have to lie down.* She was overcome by fear and anxiety. She twisted and turned in bed, feeling restless. *What I felt last night was perhaps a foreboding of things to come.* Soon her breathing became steadier; her eyes felt heavy. There wasn't much she could do other than wait for Mantoo. Absolutely tired, Nilimarani dozed off.

Mantoo rode his cycle to the hospital at break-neck speed. He even fell off his cycle a couple of times, as he was too preoccupied to notice the humps on the road. His knees were bruised, but he did not care. The bicycle's roller chain slipped off its sprockets and he lunged forward onto the handle, hitting his chest, but he felt no pain. *I have to get to the hospital as fast as I can.*

A crowd had assembled at the emergency ward by the time he reached. Mantoo's heart was racing. Huffing and puffing, he shoved his way through the crowd to the entrance of the ward. The glass door of the ward was locked from inside. Mantoo peeped in through the glass panel. There were a number of beds. Doctors and nurses were running around in a frenzy.

'I'm Anadi Samanta's son, Mantoo. Where is my father? Please let me meet him,' he shouted from behind the door.

A hospital staff opened the door. His whole body was shaking as he made his way to his father. Mantoo was ushered into a cabin and introduced to the doctor on duty. He signalled Mantoo to take a seat. The doctor got up from his seat and sat beside Mantoo. Taking a deep breath, he spoke in a rather concerned tone, 'See, your father was brought here in a very serious condition. He was senseless. He has suffered multiple fractures, muscle tears and severe injuries to his head. He was bleeding profusely from his nose when he was brought in. We are trying our best. Listen, you have to be brave and calm. I don't want to hide the truth...your father's condition is fast deteriorating. His chances of survival is...well, I must say...no better than bleak.'

He handed a document to Mantoo to sign. Suddenly, the phone on his table rang and he picked it up at once. 'Oh! I'm coming. I will be there in a second.' Saying this, the doctor hurried out of the cabin.

A minute passed, then another, then another... Mantoo's heart began to sink. He felt numb. The doctor's words pierced him like a thousand needles. He sat there, his head lowered. Two of the men who had gone to their house to inform them about the accident came running towards Mantoo on seeing him.

'So, you are here already! Good. Let's go see your father. The doctor is there by his side. Come on!' said one of them.

The man rushed out, with Mantoo close on his heels. He parted the green-linen partition of the ward and went in. Mantoo followed him in. He saw the doctor there, but a nurse was covering the patient's body with white linen. She was about to pull the sheet over the head when the doctor rushed to Mantoo and wrapped his arms around him. 'I am sorry, son, we couldn't save him.'

Mantoo could not hold his bottled-up emotions any more and burst into a loud wail. To be calm and composed at such a moment was impossible and unnatural. A couple of nurses came running into the cabin and held him by his arms, continuously rubbing his back to comfort him.

After some time, when Mantoo's wails subsided, he said to the doctor, 'Please take that cloth off his face. I want to see him.'

The doctor signalled the nurse to take the linen off and uncover the body. With a heavy heart, Mantoo rushed to the side of the body. There was blood around his lips. He lay with his mouth open and eyes closed. His legs were crumpled and there was blood everywhere. It was the most horrifying sight Mantoo had ever seen in his life. He almost fainted. He began to wail. 'Why, why, why, Father? Wake up, Father! You can't leave us like that, Father! Please, Father, please look at me. Please speak to me.'

Tenderly pulling Mantoo up from the body of his father, the doctor dragged him to his cabin and made him sit on a chair. Someone splashed some chilled water on Mantoo's face while someone else continuously rubbed his back, consoling him.

Nilimarani was awakened by incessant and impatient knocking on the door, but she couldn't open her eyes. Her head was throbbing. She tried to think straight, but was confused. She heard voices calling out to her from behind the door. *Mantoo.* Nilimarani got up with a jerk and rushed unsteadily towards the door.

She groggily opened the door. There he was—Mantoo. *But why is he alone? Where is his father?* Silence. She was confused. Her face turned blue, a thousand wrinkles appeared on her face, the twinkle in her eyes vanished, her hands dangled at her sides, her lips were pale and her hair was a mess—she was a sorry sight. Mantoo began to weep uncontrollably. His whole body shivered and he couldn't stand any more. He fell at his mother's feet.

'Mother, he is gone. He will never be with us again. I could do nothing. I was so helpless. He is dead and gone forever, Mother! He was crushed under the train. When I reached the hospital, the doctors were covering him in white cloth.'

The sound of Mantoo's wail drifted in every direction. The

neighbours, consternated, ran out of their houses and trudged down to our house to find out what the commotion was about. The children also gathered at the door on hearing the commotion. They, too, started wailing.

'Mother, are you listening? Father's gone, Mother! He will never be with us again! I could do nothing.'

Mantoo lifted his head, trying to gauge his mother's reaction. Her face was bereft of any expression. He clung to his mother's legs—they were like a log a wood. A few women held her tightly, consoling her. Mantoo shook her again and again. 'Father's dead! He has left us forever! He will never come back! Please, oh Mother, please, for God's sake, say something.'

Someone went inside the house to fetch some water and began splashing it on his mother's face. Someone rubbed her palms. After a while, she opened her eyes. She looked at Mantoo and her lips began to twitch.

Mantoo was still weeping. 'Mother, the officers asked me if they should bring the body here or if they should take him to the cremation ground from the hospital.'

She shuddered as if a bolt of lightning had struck her. One of the office staff, who had accompanied Mantoo, came forward and took out a piece of paper. It bore an undertaking written in English which needed to be signed. It would authorize the hospital management to send the body to their house or to cremate it at their end, free of charge, as the deceased was an employee of Tata Company. The man handed the paper to a woman who was holding Mother. He explained the contents of the document to the woman and pointed out where Nilimarani's signature was needed.

The officer at the hospital who had brought the document came forward and stood in front of Mother and asked her, 'Please tell us what to do? Would you like the body to be brought here or be taken to the cremation ground straight away? The body can be brought here to your house by an ambulance free of any charge, of course.'

There isn't much money at home to perform the last rites. Moreover, if the body is brought here, people will assemble, among them will be the moneylenders and it will be a great embarrassment. She took a deep breath, gathered all the strength she had left and stuttered, 'Son, th... there is no need to b...bring the body here. Let *them* cremate the body.'

Has Mother gone mad? Nilimarani's words were like a stab for Mantoo.

Pin-drop silence. Everyone present looked at each other in bewilderment. Nilimarani's heart was caught in her throat.

The man asked again, showing her the document, 'Are you sure?

Mother nodded.

'Madam, can you sign here please?' The official implored.

Mother raised her thumb, suggesting that she couldn't sign. Since the official was experienced and used to such situations, he had carried a stamp pad with him. The officer read the document aloud so that all could hear him. He then took Mother's thumb impression on the paper.

'This will do,' he said, showing the document to the gathering. 'Now I need the signatures of two witnesses,' he addressed the gathering.

Two men came forward and volunteered to sign as witnesses. The official pulled out another document that also needed Mother's thumb impression on it. It was about identifying Mantoo as the son of the deceased and authorizing him to execute all necessary documents at the hospital and at the funeral ground.

When the documentation work was complete, the official apologized to Mother, 'Madam, I am extremely sorry for this trouble, but we need to complete the formalities and the needful documentation for official record. May God give you and your children the strength to face this irreparable loss. We will make a move. Thank you.'

Mother's eyes were closed. Her mind was utterly fatigued and so was her body. She somehow managed to raise her hands and bid the officials farewell. 'God, please bless my husband with your Grace and let his soul rest in peace,' Nilimarani recited a silent prayer.

The process at the hospital was rather complicated and time-consuming. There was still some paperwork pending. There were a lot of formalities to be completed at the funeral ground. According to Hindu custom, the dead must be cremated within twenty-four hours of death and so the arrangements were swiftly underway.

The funeral ground was a lonely and desolate place. The watchman arranged for a pile of logs. A pit was dug. Meanwhile, Father's body was brought out of the ambulance van that had carried it to the funeral ground. His body was bathed and laid on a bamboo mat on the ground. There was a talisman tied to his waist by a black thread. Someone cut the thread with a knife and handed the talisman to Mantoo. What good is this now? he wondered, putting the talisman in his pocket.

When the arrangements were made, Father's body was wrapped in the mat and carried to the pyre. According to Hindu tradition, it is the duty and privilege of the eldest or youngest son to light the pyre. The priest asked Mantoo to have a bath because he wouldn't be allowed to light the pyre without proper ablutions. Mantoo obliged.

Mantoo was handed a small flare by the priest appointed by the company to help in the funeral and post-funeral rites. The priest was neither meddlesome nor stubborn, he was not fastidious about the inaccuracies in the clothing of the hapless boy and moderated the religious practice whenever he felt it warranted. As instructed by the priest, he walked round the pyre with the flare five times, said his final goodbye to Father and then touched the flare to the kindling. Mantoo, all of seventeen, stood in silence while the men around him tended the fire, turning Father's body around and poking it with a bamboo pole from time to time to facilitate the burning. Before long, the skull exploded and the men prayed loudly for the peace of his soul.

For Mantoo, it was heart-rending to see the body of the man in whose lap he had played as a kid, to see the body of the man whose hand he held as they walked in the park, to see the body of the man who was his father and to see the body of the man he loved, disintegrating before his eyes. A shattered self and a bleeding heart he was. Mantoo tried to gather those broken pieces within his heart.

A strange sadness descended on him as the memories of his father and of his life with him drifted in, falling and rising like the tide. 'It is alright, son, we have to keep moving!' said a voice from somewhere far.

When the ashes cooled, a handful was placed in a brass jar and handed over to Mantoo for immersion in the Holy Ganges.

Mantoo returned to the hospital along with the hospital staff in the ambulance. He picked up his bicycle and pedalled all the way home, the memory of the funeral still haunting him, the overwhelming smell of burning flesh still fresh in his mind.

It was almost sunset when Mantoo reached home. Images from the past haunted him. Father and son used to walk together in Jubilee Park and gossip during leisurely nights. He would listen to him telling stories with rapt attention—stories that transported him to distant horizons. *It still doesn't feel like Father is gone. He is somewhere beyond the setting sun.* He looked at the sky, letting out a sigh. *Now all I have left is memories.*

As he alighted from his bicycle at the gate of their quarter, the sky turned a deep grey. His legs were stiff, muscles tired. The clothes he wore felt damp and they clung to his body. The house looked forlorn. His heart began to beat faster. *How can I face Mother? What lies in store for our family? What conspiracy is destiny hatching against us?*

He dreaded the night. The sight of the funeral pyre consuming his father's body flashed in his mind. The smell of burning wood and flesh still lingered in his mind.

His heart sank as he approached the front door of their house—a house that was built so lovingly by his parents. He longed for the comfort of his mother's lap. He longed to go into a deep sleep so that it could free him of the smell of burning wood and flesh that still haunted him.

He rolled the bicycle in and leaned it against the wall close to the porch. The image of his mother loomed in his mind. She was in a whirl when he last left the house for the hospital. His mother was his life and Father his pride. Every time he fell down, his mother would help him up, dust him and encourage him to keep walking.

Mantoo did not want to disturb his mother, so he gently knocked on the door. A neighbour opened it. He entered the room and went straight to the courtyard. There, he dug a hole in the ground and placed the brass urn containing his father's ashes. He covered the hole with earth. He prostrated on the ground and, as instructed by the priest, prayed, 'Father, may your soul rest in peace.'

He returned to the room. His mother was lying there on her bed laid on the floor. A couple of women from the neighbourhood sat around her. Her eyes were closed. Her legs, limp and frail, were stretched out. She was in a plain white saree, her wrists were bereft of any bangles and the vermilion on her forehead had been wiped off. Noticing all these signs of his mother's widowhood, Mantoo plunged into his mother's lap and wept aloud. 'Mother, I have set fire to his body with my own hands, here look at them, Mother, these very hands. I couldn't save him, forgive me, Mother. His body turned into smoke and mingled with the air. His voice will no longer reach us, nor will he hear us. Before lighting the funeral pyre, I looked at his face. He looked so peaceful, as if he was only sleeping...'

Neelmarani's chest tightened and her eyes filled with tears. Mantoo's brothers and sisters too rushed to their mother and began crying. The three-month-old baby also started crying in her bed. Their father had been like a banyan tree, giving shade and shelter. He always stood like a column of light when darkness engulfed the family.

Nilimarani quickly realized how heartbroken her son was. Quickly straightening herself, she pulled Mantoo to her bosom. 'Fate has been very unkind to him. His life has been one of unremitting toil. God has relieved his soul of misery,' she mumbled.

'Where is Father?' Trupti asked.

Mantoo looked at her and gestured towards the sky, 'Heaven.'

'How far is heaven from here?'

Nilimarani closed her eyes and tears rolled down her cheeks.

7

I CANNOT AFFORD TO FAIL

Some events change the course of our lives forever—for good or for worse.

The death of our father was the most profound and life-altering event for us. The bereavement was traumatic. That fateful day, Mother sat with her head thrown back against the hard wall, almost motionless, except for when some thought came to her mind and she sobbed like a baby that cries itself to sleep.

That day seemed never-ending and the night even longer. The children slept in silence and discomfort as their bones creaked from emotional exhaustion. The family would have gone to bed on an empty stomach had some kind neighbours not brought in some food. A deathly silence fell over the entire house. The people paying them visits to offer their condolences tried to console them.

'Everybody loses a parent, an aunt or an uncle, or a grandparent when they grow very old.'

'Some people die in accidents, like your father.'

'Some people lose their lives to a deadly disease.'

'It is heartbreaking to lose someone so close and dear to you, but you have to go on with your life, dear.'

Nilimarani was not able to catch any sleep that night. She was in a state of anguish all through the night, tossing and turning in her bed. She remembered the minutest detail of their life together, the ones she always overlooked but now revealed themselves in their entirety. She did not touch a morsel of food the previous day and the previous night. She simply sat in one place with her gaze locked on something somewhere very far, and she hardly responded to anything that was happening around her. Her head ached. Her thoughts oscillated between the present and the past, between Kalarabanka and Jamshedpur. Once in a while she looked around the room—the faint moonlight flowed in through the half-open window, as if guarding the family and consoling the grieving souls.

Morning dawned, but the gloom still lingered in the room. The sun was up but was struggling to push its comforting rays to the earth through the inimical clouds. Nilimarani mustered the strength to get up and go to the window. From there, she could see the market square gearing up for the day ahead. The treetops in front of the house were aquiver, the depressing breath of rain hung in the air. In the street yonder, a peddler cried his wares. The faint note of a song playing on a public address system somewhere in the distance reached her ears. At forty, Nilimarani still looked beautiful and calm, except for the lines of worry and agony that showed on her forehead. Despite those lines, her face bore an expression of unflinching strength. Her dull gaze was fixed on the patches of the blue sky.

The newspaper-boy delivered Father's favourite newspaper, *The Samaja*, as usual, but it lay sluggishly on the foreground, waiting to be picked up.

Life outside the house went on as usual—people rushing to work, children running to school, vehicles whizzing past. Things, however, were never the same for us after that day. Life had taken a complete U-turn. The rooms weren't cleaned; they were dusty, with pieces of broken hearts and broken lives strewn everywhere.

The umbrella that had offered protection to the family during rain and shine was broken, dismembered and consumed by the rising flames of the funeral pyre. My mother grieved not only the physical loss of her companion but also the loss of dreams and expectations that they shared, the loss of possibilities, of might-have-beens.

Something was coming to get her. She felt an uncanny dread in her heart. What was it? She did not have an answer, but she felt it, creeping towards her through the sounds, the scents and the colours that filled the air. Her bosom rose and fell tumultuously. She began to recognize this entity approaching to possess her and she strove to push it back with all her will. *I have to live alone with my children, for my children. I will resist every powerful will that is imposed on me, a widow.*

My mother was not a kind of person to go on mourning. Sad beyond words though she was, she knew she had to be resilient and stern—for herself, for her children. This is not the end of the world, she kept telling herself. She realized that her priorities in life had changed. I have to bring up my children single-handedly. This is no time to be heartbroken, she resolved.

Nilimarani buckled up to face the challenges. She knew she would have to brave obstacles at every step of the way. Father's death was not something she had foreseen; fate had kept it hidden from her. She knew that rough times do come, but they blow away with time—like the clouds, letting the sunlight in. *My children too will grow up and settle down. This house with light up with the laughter of my grandchildren one day.*

She begun to look at life with an entirely different perspective; her own survival as well as that of her children were of paramount importance. *I have to pull myself through this.*

That evening, seeing his mother brooding, Mantoo crawled over to where she stood by the window. He gently tugged at her saree and she turned around. Wiping her tears that refused to stop, she sat down. Mantoo buried his head in her lap and she ran her slender fingers through his hair. The tangled curls of myriad thoughts in his head began to untangle and ease out. Gently, she queried about the proceedings at the hospital and if the funeral was carried out properly. They didn't get to converse the previous day. The sight of the blood stains on his father's body and on his clothes still haunted Mantoo; his vision, even in his wakeful state, was besprinkled with that scarlet horror. He slowly narrated everything to her, the memory still fresh and painful, like a raw wound. They couldn't hold back their tears any more.

'We have to survive. His soul will rest in peace when he watches us make it through this together. Things will not be the same. You will have to buckle up and lend me a hand,' Mother mumbled, wiping her tears and Mantoo's too.

'You are right, Mother!' said Mantoo, his voice trembling. 'We have to get through these trying times, together.'

Mantoo recollected his father's last, and final, words to him before leaving for Cuttack: 'Take care of everything at home, Mantoo! Help your mother! I'll see you tomorrow, son!'

How could I not see his despair? Mantoo cursed himself. The trip to Cuttack was an unexpected one and Father was not very eager to make it. But he was duty-bound to fulfill his social obligations as a son-in-law, as a husband. 'I'll see you tomorrow, son!' His father's last words kept ringing in his ears. A tomorrow that was never to come.

'What did you go through when you heard the news, Mother?' Mantoo asked.

Nilimarani leaned against the wall. She knew why her son had raised such a question. She knew what was going on in Mantoo's tender mind. Losing a parent, bidding them goodbye for good is always difficult, but all the more so when you are young. At first, she hesitated. He is perhaps going through the same emotions I did when I lost my mother, she thought to herself. It is like losing one's own self.

Despite her unwillingness to answer the question, she began comforting him. It was time for her to take on the role of a counsellor. After all, being the eldest, he would have to shoulder the responsibility of the family soon. She spoke about how she felt when her mother passed away. She was only sixteen then and everything happened right in front of her eyes. The burden of looking after her siblings, especially her small brother and her father fell on her tender shoulders.

The conversation between her and Mantoo reminded her of the conversation she had had with her grandmother when she was young. The advice she got from her helped her through the trying times in life, especially the financial setback that they suffered.

'No matter how much time we get with our parents, it always seems less. We know that we might outlive our parents, but that does not take the suffering and the sense of loss away.'

Her words soothed Mantoo's troubled mind. He felt the heavy cloud that shrouded his heart dissipating. Suddenly, Mantoo remembered the talisman that was found on his father's body while it was being bathed at the funeral ground. He pulled it out from his pocket and showed it to his mother. 'This is what we found on him as his body was being bathed at the funeral ground. Mother, did you know that Father had this on him? What was it for? Should we keep it?'

Mother looked at it, raised her head and closed her eyes, as if recollecting something from the seemingly bottomless chasm of her memory. The day Father had narrated his chance meeting with a certain baba flashed in her mind. After hearing her husband's narration, she had said, 'Oh, we don't know what's in store for us, but if we walk hand in hand with our chin up, we can face any trouble head-on. However, I cannot bear to see you wasting your life like this.' Her voice sounded so confident.

'Yes, I know he used to wear this talisman,' she said, her eyes still closed and her voice heavy. 'He wore it because some baba had predicted that he would meet with an untimely death. The talisman couldn't protect him. Fate won. His rigorous penances didn't help him.' She narrated how my father met that baba and why he did the penance with such dedication. 'There is no need to keep it. Just take it away from my sight!' she said, slightly irritated. 'Throw them all,' she said, pointing towards Father's puja set-up, 'in the Subarnarekha River when you go there for the tenth-day rituals.'

Mantoo walked to the corner and placed the talisman on the wooden platform, in front of which his father sat every morning and worshipped. Suddenly, there was a rap on the door. They looked at each other, puzzled. *Who could that be?* They were not expecting anyone.

Mantoo went to the door and opened it. Some women of the neighbourhood trooped in with several bowls in their hands. Sitting down beside Mother, one of them said, 'Sister Nilima, don't worry about food, we will bring it to you till you are fit enough to cook on your own. Is there anything else you need? Please don't hesitate to tell us. We shall do our best. Oh yes, here is some money, the entire neighbourhood has raised it for you. Accept it, you may need it!'

Nilimarani's face began to burn with shame. The women had asked her, the previous day, why she hadn't wanted her husband's body to be brought home. She had shared her plight with them in good faith. *We need this money. This help is indeed godsend.* She felt grateful. 'Thank you, sister, it was so kind and thoughtful of you all. God bless you!' she said, accepting the money. Her eyes moistened. She took the free end of her saree and wiped her tears.

The children were really hungry. They had barely had anything to eat in two days. Mantoo signalled his younger sister to serve the food. She brought bowls to the middle of the room and asked her younger brother to get the plates. There was enough food in the bowls, enough for two good meals for all. The children had a sumptuous meal and soon fell asleep.

Mantoo still did not know why his mother had refused to bring his father's body home for cremation and the question was killing him. Unable to take it any longer, he asked his mother, 'Why did you ask the officer not to bring father's body home?' His eyes were moist again.

Mother took a deep breath, looked at Mantoo straight in his eyes and said in a voice that bore a tone of lividness, 'I didn't have a barrel of money. Had I asked the body to be brought home, a lot of people would have gathered. We would have to observe all the rituals and that would have needed money. I did not have a single penny on me. How do you think we would have managed that? I agree that my proposition must have sounded ludicrous and harsh, but I had no choice. But how would anybody know my plight? It was good that the company authorities arranged everything at their end and paid for it too. A million thanks to them!'

That conversation was an eye-opener. Mantoo felt slightly embarrassed. He developed a new-found admiration for his mother's presence of mind even in her state of utter desperateness and grief. I have to be their strength and support now, he resolved.

'Mother, I will start distributing newspapers from tomorrow if you allow me. I'm going to speak to that hawker today. You can start making cow-dung cakes again. The priest who performed Father's last rites has asked me to come to the Subarnarekha bank on the tenth day for the final rituals. He may charge something. Keep this money with you. We will need it. We also need to perform the eleventh- and twelfth-day rituals.'

'Yes, but what about your Class XI examinations? They will start in two days, isn't it?'

'I'll manage somehow. I will not miss my papers,' replied Mantoo, his voice resolute.

'OK, but you mustn't neglect your studies. Do you remember how angry your father was when he came to know about your newspaper-delivering venture? He expected so much more from you that—'

The mother-son conference was disturbed by the creaking sound of the gate. Mantoo rushed to look out of the window. It was his mother's sister's husband. He rushed back to Mother and whispered, 'It's our older uncle.'

A few more lines appeared on her forehead. Nilimarani began adjusting her saree. When she was done tidying up, Mantoo rushed out to open the door. He greeted his uncle and ushered him in. Mother didn't seem to like his coming and gave him a sidelong glance. He sat there near the door, as he didn't want to come in. His face was heavy with apprehension that they would ask for financial help. He sat silently, impatience obvious on his face; probably trying to figure out where to begin. Neither did Mother say anything. The children too were not interested in talking to him. Finally, he took a deep breath and addressed my mother, 'Sister, I'm sorry I couldn't come yesterday. I was unwell. I still haven't recovered, but I had to come anyhow. I know this must be very hard for you. But who can stop the onslaught of fate, right?'

Mother glared at him for she was familiar with his snobbery. She knew that he had feigned illness. He was only trying to put up a smokescreen to conceal the truth. Such an unsympathetic and uncompassionate guy, Mother thought to herself. Not paying a visit the previous day was unacceptable. If he had any regard for his brother-in-law, he would have come the previous day and stayed with Mantoo to console him at the hospital and at the funeral ground. He was the senior-most member of the family after Father in the city.

She chose not to react. He was aware of our family's financial condition and he perhaps feared that he might need to help us out with the rites.

Uncle continued, 'Actually, I have come to ask when you will be able to repay the ₹5,000 that Big Brother [Father] had borrowed from me. I don't want to chase you for that, but I would appreciate it if you can give me a date, not very far though, according to your convenience. I will come back to you on that day. You needn't worry about the interest; I don't mean to burden you more for I know how hard-pressed you must be. I am more concerned about the principal. You must be knowing how hard it is to earn money.'

My mother lost her patience. *Why did Mantoo's father have to approach this man of all people for such a hefty loan?* She wasn't convinced that her brother-in-law was telling the truth.

'Brother-in-law,' she said, 'I am aware that you are not the best of people. However, I didn't expect you to stoop this low. As you are aware, I was not privy to the transaction you had with my husband. He is gone now and has become one with the earth. Even if what you say is true, I am in no position to repay you. If you have any humanity left in you, please be gone at once. If ever I have money to spare, I will surely repay your loan after finding out how genuine your claim is. Thank you for coming.' She turned her face away.

Mother's subtle and artful insinuation enraged him, his face turned red. He swallowed hard and then said with a smirk, 'Sister, your father was witness to that transaction. You should talk to him. I want my money back.'

Mother refused to waste another moment on her brother-in-law. She didn't say anything, nor did Uncle, who sat there for a couple of minutes before rushing out of the house.

People kept pouring in through the day to pay their condolences. Among them were father's colleagues, our neighbours and other acquaintances from Jamshedpur and Kalarabanka. Around four in the evening, a couple of men stood at their doorstep. They were Afghan moneylenders (kabuliwala). Mantoo froze. In the meanwhile, Mother, too, came to the door and stood beside her son. Her worst fear had come true.

The moneylenders greeted Mother very politely and expressed their condolences. Mother didn't reply, nor did she think it proper to return their greetings.

'Look, madam, we are moneylenders, your husband had taken loans from us. Here is the receipt. Please tell us when we should come by again to collect the principal. Don't worry about the "interest" part; we have collectively decided to waive it off considering your husband's sudden demise.'

Mother had an inkling that Father was borrowing from moneylenders. One day, she confronted him about it, but Father brushed the topic aside.

These men have no business knocking at my door and talking to me—a penniless widow—about transactions they had with my husband. If I don't shoo these wolves away, they will come again and again.

'Do you think you can twist my arm because I am a widow? Was I privy to your transactions with my husband? I have no information that my husband owes you anything and I don't care if he did. The man you had given a loan to is gone forever. And let me tell you, he has not left a penny for us. So, please go away. And don't you dare pester me or my children again.'

They stood there with their heads lowered. Mother shouted again, 'Go away. Do you hear me? I will turn you over to the police for harassing a widow!' Her confidence overwhelmed them. They slithered away in silence. She banged the door shut behind them and turning to Mantoo said, 'DON'T open the door to any strangers.'

Nilimarani resolved not to waste another moment lamenting and mourning. Mantoo started his newspaper delivery venture. Every morning, he woke up at five and biked up to Sakchi bus stand. He helped the newspaper distributor in sorting the papers area-wise, an additional work for which he got extra payment on the spot.

By the time he returned home, it would be eight in the morning. After having some breakfast, which comprised rice flakes soaked in water and jaggery, and after a little chit-chat with Mother, he would settle down to study. He had his papers every alternate day except on the holidays. His exams were scheduled in the afternoon. He didn't deliver papers on the days he had to perform the tenth-, eleventh- and twelfth-day rituals. He slogged with his studies till late at night. There was only one room in the quarter. The family went to sleep and the light had to be switched off. So he studied in the kitchen.

One day, he told Mother, 'Mother, I am sometimes unable to concentrate. Every time I close my eyes to revise the chapters, I see Father's face, and the whole scene at the hospital and the funeral ground flashes in my mind. My concentration is failing me. How can I sit for the examination?'

Mother could understand his concern. Anybody in his situation would naturally be vulnerable. She counselled him, 'Son, life is about marching forward. The past will only push you into a dungeon. Look at your brothers and sisters! They look up to you and me. You can't afford to be faint-hearted, my dear son! You can do it.' Mother knew he was at a crucial juncture; either he would gather himself together or scatter. 'You are my only hope now.' She caressed Mantoo's hair.

Armed with his mother's confidence in him, Mantoo said, 'I have to make it.'

The post-funeral ablution rituals were minimized. On Mantoo's request, the priest, a kind-hearted fellow, hastened the ritual process enabling Mantoo to appear for the examinations. During the ten days of mourning, the neighbours supplied wheat flour, rice and pulses—a common practice in Hindu societies.

The examinations were over by the end of March 1969 and the results were to be out by June. Mantoo had the entire day to himself and there was nothing much to do back at home during this time. He decided to take up a job so as to earn a little more to support the family. The newspaper distributor for whom Mantoo worked had a book shop and a stationery store. Mantoo asked him if he needed a hand in his shop. The distributor indeed was looking for a salesman for his bookstore. When he offered the job to Mantoo, he agreed at once.

The income earned by Mantoo and Mother was meager, yet they somehow managed a simple meal. The neighbours stopped sending them supplies at my mother's request. Mantoo's younger sister dropped out of school since studies never interested her. She chose to stay at home and help her mother in her cow-dung cake business instead.

We continued to live in the quarter. And then the unexpected happened. One day, a few officials from the Tata Company came with a notice asking us to vacate the house, as it was an official quarter. That news was like a bolt out of the blue. The quarter was our home for almost nineteen years. My mother's heart sank. The officials realized mother's consternation and spoke softly, 'Don't worry too much, madam. The company has allowed you a month's time to look for an alternative.' Both Mantoo and my mother were relieved to hear that and quickly nodded in agreement.

On the flip side, the officers had some good news to share. They informed us that the company was processing the paperwork for term insurance and an ex gratia payment from the company. The news gave some respite to my mother's frayed nerves. The whole process was expected to take some three months.

After the officers were gone, Mother and Brother settled down for yet another talk. Since Nilimarani could not afford to pay house rent, she decided to leave Jamshedpur and return to the village, bag and baggage. She mentally prepared herself to again start living in that humble hut. *Life in Jamshedpur was a pleasant distraction from the village life.*

Mantoo sat watching his mother's face. He knew she was making up her mind about something. 'What is on your mind, Mother?'

She turned towards Mantoo and peered into his eyes with intense silence. She suppressed her expression. Suddenly, she burst into tears.

'Are...are you okay?' He asked, hesitating.

She stretched her hand and stroked his hair. 'Together, we have to take care of everything.' She blurted out, without meaning to say it. He didn't understand what she meant by that, but he nodded with assurance. She closed her eyes and rested her head against the wall. 'I left the village almost two decades ago. That feels like a lifetime. The thought of returning is making me feel a little nervous, that's all,' she said.

Mantoo was surprised to hear his mother's decision, but he nodded understandingly.

The memory of her life in the village was beginning to fade. She knew that once she went back to the village, she would be the topic of all gossip. Her pairing with Anadi Samanta would be questioned. Why wasn't she married off to an affluent family? they would ask. She would be judged.

She wasn't willing to live with anybody: her father or her sisters. She wanted to live her life on her own terms. She had to fulfill all of her husband's dreams including his dream of renovating the village house.

People would talk, talk behind her back, but she wouldn't go around silencing them. She resolved to brave the storm. She would have to bear it all in her stride. She was a realist to the core.

My mother's younger sister was married to the teacher of a local school in Jamshedpur. He was also from Kalarabanka. He worked in the same school where Mantoo studied, but my mother did not get along well with her. She was very proud of her husband and the money that he amassed by conducting private tuitions. She and her husband always looked down upon my parents. My uncle and aunt never visited us.

When my aunt heard that my mother was contemplating returning to the village, she came running to her one day. She discouraged the idea. She feared that once Nilimarani landed in the village, she would narrate how they didn't stand by her side. Their father would get angry and not give them any share of their ancestral property. She tried to justify her stand by saying that the town was a land of opportunities and the village wasn't.

'In case you wish to stay at Father's homestead instead of that dingy house of your in-laws, it might antagonize our brother, who is yet to settle down and is the natural heir. He is the family's blue-eyed boy. I suppose usurping his prospects in life will be rather unbecoming of you...'

'Gracious God! Your thoughts are ridiculously theatrical. I don't care what you think about me and what I decide,' said my mother, exasperated.

It was I who brought to her the proposal of marriage from her in-laws' side. How can she even think that I will live off my father? Your husband's house is your real home. She remembered her mother's words. *I have to go back to the village, to my husband's house.*

Nilimarani's youngest sister visited her another day. 'Please stay here till things settle down. Mantoo will get a job at the Tata Company when he turns eighteen,' her sister pleaded with her. Though the third sister was her pet, Nilimarani turned down her offer very lovingly and politely.

As she sat thinking, about what awaited her in the village and her sisters' counselling, she had a vision about her in-laws' house. It was the smallest homestead in the village. The house may be small but it should suffice my family, she told herself.

My paternal grandfather had recently passed away. My father got the message of Grandfather's demise very late. Telegraph services were not available in the village yet or in the closest post office at Raghunathpur.

My eldest sister, who had been living in the village with our grandparents ever since she was ten months old, performed the funeral rituals. Of course, my father reached the village two days later and completed the remaining rituals.

After my grandfather's death, my sister was all alone in the house. She didn't feel like cooking even though she had all provisions in the house. She managed by eating flattened rice soaked in water with chopped onions and green chillies. A day after my father had left for Jamshedpur, my maternal grandfather visited my sister. Seeing her plight, he took her to his house and asked her to live with them.

After the death of my grandparents, there was no one to take care of the house. Even my father's aunt had passed away. My father always harboured the dream of renovating his house, but unfortunately never had the means to do it. Returning to the village at that time was not a feasible option too. After all, he had a steady job in Jamshedpur.

My mother started making preparations to go back to the village. At that time, she did not have enough money to buy tickets to her village. The schools were in session and her school-going children would have to continue till the examinations were over. She also had to wait until she got the insurance claim and the ex gratia money.

After a month of her receiving the notice to vacate the house, a man turned up at their doorstep. He looked like he was in his thirties. He claimed that the quarter where we were currently living, had been allocated to him and he had come to see the house. He produced the allocation letter from the company. Upon hearing our desperate condition, he allowed us to continue staying in the house till we left for the village, which, the man guessed, would be shortly.

In the meanwhile, my mother received another notice from the company. It mentioned that unless she vacated the house, she would not be paid the ex gratia that was due to her. Therefore, on the last day of the notice period, Mantoo went to the office and submitted an application stating that we have vacated the house. The new allottee gave them the quarter occupation certificate, which they submitted in the company.

During the first week of June 1969, Nilimarani and Mantoo were summoned to the personnel department of Tata Company. When they reached the office, they were handed the ex gratia money of ₹5,000 and the insurance claim money of ₹20,000. We started making preparations for our return to the village.

It was the second Sunday of June 1969. We woke up at five o'clock. The neighbourhood was quiet and the moon was still floating like a pearl in a pool of ink. In the half-light, the house looked less familiar and sadder. The packing was done. The old and rusted trunks were pulled out of the top shelf in the room and whatever knick-knacks we had were emptied into them, along with our clothes and bedding.

Mantoo had finished delivering papers for the day. He took a half-day off from the bookstore. He was home in time for lunch. Mantoo would be missing mother's loving care and affection. He was staying back to take up his father's job. He was sulky and silent all through lunch. When we retired to the room after helping Mother with the dishes, cleaning the kitchen and packing the utensils and crockeries in a wooden carton, Mantoo went to Mother and rested his head on her lap.

'I can't believe that this time tomorrow we will be in our village, we will be with your grandfather and your sister.' Her gaze was fixed at some undefined point in the ceiling while her fingers caressed Mantoo's ruffled hair.

'Mother, how will life be in the village?'

'We don't know anyone there in the village other than Grandfather and Big Sister.'

'Who shall we play with?'

'Why did we not go to the village during the vacations?'

The children had never been to the village and therefore they had no idea what to expect and had many questions to ask their mother.

On our last day in Jamshedpur, the weather was hot and dry. As we were lounging in the room after a sumptuous lunch, enjoying the summer breeze, an ice cream vendor passed by, shouting his ware. We insisted on having ice creams and Mother couldn't say no. When our father was alive, he took us out for an ice cream treat every Sunday. She knew that such treats would be unavailable in the village.

We were to take the 7 p.m. bus. As the clock struck 4 p.m., our neighbours started trickling in in ones, twos, threes and fours to bid us farewell. Some brought with them chocolates and others brought biscuits and bread. My mother was ever grateful for the help and support that she received from her neighbours after Father's untimely demise. 'I will always remember you and be grateful for all that you have done for us,' she told them.

The sun was about to set in the horizon and the evening sky was painted in beautiful shades of orange and purple. My mother looked up at the sky. *I had my whole life planned with someone I called husband. I made sacrifices for him. I did things I wouldn't normally. He gave me a family to call my own, and yet one fine morning, he simply vanished into thin air, leaving everything on my shoulders.* My mother started sobbing. She wiped her tears and went back to check the rooms and soon returned to check her luggage. Suddenly, they heard a knock on the door, a light tap. Mantoo looked out of the window. It was the would-be occupant of the house, and he was accompanied by our immediate neighbour—an aunt we all adored. Mantoo opened the door and ushered them in.

The would-be occupant of the quarter was very sad when he learned about my mother's decision to relocate to her native village, leaving Mantoo behind to fend for himself.

'Dear sister, if I may be allowed to address you so, I know how you must be feeling having to say goodbye to this town, where you have lived for a quarter of a century.' He added, taking a glance at Mantoo, 'Poor young man! What is to become of him when you all are gone? The poor boy will be all alone. I will not mind it if he chooses to stay with me in this house. It is not right that he should be living alone at this tender age. I cannot picture a more wretched condition as his. Besides, his Class XI results will be out soon. I leave it to you and Mantoo to decide,' he said in all earnestness.

Mother couldn't believe her ears at first. She had mixed feelings about it. She looked at her neighbour to check if what she heard the man say was for real. Our neighbour nodded. She even expressed her appreciation for Mantoo's conduct and enterprising spirit. This is perhaps how God opens one door when He closes another, my mother thought to herself. Her heart melted with gratitude.

'Mantoo may continue to live in this house for a couple of months more or even longer, as my family will be a little delayed in joining me here. I have some land in the village and my wife has been looking after the cultivation. And she won't be joining me until we find a share-cropper. Besides that, my parents are also getting old and they need to be taken care of,' the would-be occupant quickly added.

'I wouldn't mind if I should be permitted to cook the meals for both of us in lieu of the rent payable by me towards this free lodging and boarding,' Mantoo said.

'It's a done deal,' the would-be occupant said putting his hand on Mantoo's shoulders.

'Then it is quite fortunate that Mantoo will continue to stay here in the quarter which has been his home for the last fifteen years,' Mother's tone was laced with happiness *Oh, this man is an angel!* She wished Mantoo all the very best and hugged him goodbye.

Bidding goodbye to the town and leaving her eldest son behind was not easy for Nilimarani. She grew nostalgic. *When I was married, I was only sixteen. I was almost twenty-three when we moved to Jamshedpur. This is the place where I experienced a new life, a new life with my husband. Back in the village, I was either someone's daughter or a daughter-in-law and my husband was always away. I am carrying so many memories of this place and my life here with me.*

Her moist eyes shifted towards her eldest son, who stood by Mother's side at the bus station, waiting to bid her goodbye. Mantoo touched Mother's feet. And with a heavy heart, we left for the village.

Nilimarani took the ladies seat in the bus. A young lady was seated by the window. They exchanged glances. She had a very attractive face.

'Where are you going?' asked my mother, trying to start a conversation.

'Baripada,' she replied. 'And where are you going?'

'Cuttack. From there, we will take a bus to our village, Kalarabanka,' Mother replied adjusting her hold on her baby daughter in her lap.

'So, it is vacation time and you plan to visit your near and dear ones, right?' The lady was curious.

We never availed any vacation. She felt a little embarrassed. 'No, not exactly, actually I am moving to my native village.'

The woman looked at her inquisitively and asked. 'How long have you lived in Jamshedpur?'

'Oh, many years,' she counted on her fingers. 'Almost two decades.'

'Oh, that's a long time. But why are you relocating? Please forgive me if I sound intrusive.'

'Well, I lost my husband in an accident a couple of months ago. I am relocating to my native village to start my life once again.'

'I'm so sorry, sister, I didn't mean—'

'Oh dear, it's alright, you don't have to apologize! What has happened, has happened, you or I can't change our destiny, dear, can we?'

Mother looked at her. She had drops of tears in the corners of her eyes, just about to roll down.

'Why are you crying, sister?

'Three months back I lost my husband too.'

'How…?'

'He worked as a workman in the blast-furnace section. I used to be a stay-home mom. One day, he didn't come home from work. He was on his morning shift. His duty was to get over by 2 p.m. When he didn't return till four, I assumed he was doing overtime. I waited for the next shift to be over. I waited at the doorstep for several hours; still, he didn't show up.'

The woman took a pause to wipe her tears and continued, 'I began to worry. Hours passed and soon it was 10 p.m. My heart sank. I didn't know what to do. So I went to my neighbour's house. When he heard my plight, he immediately rushed to the plant on his bicycle and assured me that he would be back with my husband.'

'My husband was a teetotaler. He usually returned home straight after his duty got over. I thought he was perhaps tired doing double shifts and hence must have slept off in the retiring room. I was tired of waiting. My neighbour returned early in the morning, it was still dark. What he told us took my breath away and I fainted.' The woman was choking. My mother pulled her in a tight embrace and soon she regained her composure.

She continued, 'Molten iron from the furnace, instead of going into the molds, suddenly spilled onto the floor of the plant and my husband was caught unaware. Within seconds, he was completely engulfed in the fiery hot molten iron. He died on the spot. It took very long to extricate the charred remains of his body. They didn't send the body home fearing that I might not be able to sustain the shock.' The woman took some time to catch her breath before she continued her story, 'The company arranged for the funeral. My parents had come. My neighbour sent a message to them through the bus driver of the Tata-Baripada bus. I have two daughters. One is seven years old and the other, four. I came here yesterday with my father, who is seated behind. Today I had to sign some papers for insurance claim settlement and I am returning to my parental home.'

A silence of grief befell both the women. They kept wiping their tearful eyes, taking care not to draw attention. By about midnight, the bus reached Bahadagoda. The driver parked the bus in front of a roadside restaurant for the passengers to have dinner. We ate the biscuits and chocolates that our neighbours had given us.

Mother felt sad for the woman but had her own realization too; her experience was not the worst after all. She felt a strange wave of relief and was filled with a renewed sense of confidence. She was not the only one going through such an ordeal. She didn't need to see where she'd been, only where she was going.

For Nilimarani, returning to the village was like returning to the place her heart called 'home'. Destiny was bringing them to the village after twenty-long years. Nilimarani let out a sigh as she alighted from the bus at the Kalarabanka bus stop.

My eldest sister came to the bus stop in Grandfather's bullock-cart to fetch us all to the village. She ran to Mother and hugged her. Mother too took her in a tight embrace.

By the time we arrived at Grandfather's homestead, it was almost mid-day. 'Ah, here we are! This is your grandfather's place, children,' Nilimarani announced. The memories of her childhood came back to her. She sneaked a glance at the garden from under the veil. Visions of the nimble-footed Sefali, romping and playing with her friends in the garden, flashed in her mind. The swing, her favourite spot in the garden, was not visible; perhaps it had been pulled down after she got married. A sudden surge of the thrill of swinging in the air rushed through her body. She quickly surveyed the garden. It looked forlorn and almost barren, much of the vegetation was gone; some wild bushes could be seen growing along the fences, threatening to invade the garden where once many flowering and fruit trees grew. A coconut tree trunk lay covered by a cushion of moss. The cheerless sight of the garden saddened her. The house too looked worn out and the ambiance was at best insipid. She solemnly wished her mother was alive—she would have come running to receive her, taken her in a warm embrace. She fought back the tears that had begun to well up. She collected the free end of her saree and wiped her eyes. Taking a couple of deep breaths, she gathered herself to face the situation that was waiting to unfold before her.

The news of Father's death spread like wildfire in the village and so, upon our arrival, there was a huge crowd outside our house. Mother felt a little awkward. She had come to the village after a gap of about two decades, for the first time since she left for Jamshedpur. The village was the same as it was then; nothing had changed in two decades. There were whispers and murmurs.

Becoming a widow is the worst thing to happen to a woman, especially if the husband is the family's only breadwinner. Widows usually get stigmatized. These helpless women are often neglected and mistreated. Sometimes, they are even evicted from their own homes. In fact, this was one of the main reasons why Mother decided to return to the village, to prevent someone else from claiming our father's house. Poverty was again another weakness that often consigned widows to unspeakable sufferings at the hands of greedy family members.

My mother had acquired a new place in the society, that of a widow. And if that wasn't enough, there was the emptiness in her life after Father's death. I will have to face the social restrictions and alienation that comes with widowhood, she thought to herself. Her own relatives and neighbours would shun her. She would no longer be invited to social functions. She would have to turn vegan. She would need to observe several religious rituals. For a year, she would neither be allowed to enter anybody's house nor would they come to visit her. Men, newlyweds and pregnant women would not receive food prepared in our house or served by her.

'You will have to return to your husband's house. This house ceased to be yours the day you got married,' someone said.

Oh, this isolation is a boon in disguise, Mother thought to herself. She needed some alone time to mourn. *Aagh, this stupidity!* Her progressive mind revolted. Someday, I will stand for change, she resolved.

She looked back. The children were unloading the baggage from the cart. The focus of the crowd shifted to the children. Somebody caressed the heads of the younger kids, others, women mostly, hugged them. The kids were embarrassed.

Suddenly a new sensation distracted her, a hand softly landed on her shoulder and rested. A male voice, pleasant and reassuring, one that she was well acquainted with, told her: 'Nilima, welcome home.' It was her father's voice.

She walked through the vestibule, to the courtyard and sat down on the porch. Tears were still rolling down her cheeks which she tried her level best to restrain. She dabbed the tears off her cheek with the free end of her saree.

Do people think that I am weak, that I am broken? Am I an object of people's pity? Her mind throbbed to find an answer. Her eyes were moist. She decided to ignore what was happening around her. *I'm strong. I have a mission to accomplish and I cannot afford to be frail.* She kept telling herself.

My grandfather, who sat beside her on the porch, sullen, suddenly ventured to ask, 'How did it all happen, dear?'

The question rekindled the pain and the memories that she was trying so hard to bury, to push back to the deeper recesses of the mind. *What is it that he wants to know? What is it that he doesn't know?* Questions like these troubled her. She didn't say a word. She looked at the point of the floor in front of her toes in order to avoid her father's probing gaze. A couple of teardrops found their way on to the floor. It took her a moment before she could speak. Even then, her voice was just a breath. She uttered a single sentence, 'I lost him, Father...' She could say no more. She got up at once and went inside the room, laid on the bare floor and began to sob. It was only later that she narrated the whole thing, in as much detail as she could, to her father.

The next morning, Mother woke up early and so did we. The sun was rising in the eastern horizon, but the sun rays were yet to reach the courtyard; a mild breeze gently caressed our bare skin. Breakfast at Grandfather's house was rather doleful. Nobody seemed to have much of an appetite that morning. We prepared to go to our father's ancestral house. Grandfather wasn't too convinced about Mother's decision to move there. He wanted her to stay on in his homestead for a few more days. She did not want to compromise on her values and what she had set out to achieve. Goodbyes are sometimes inevitable.

Mother left the youngest of us in the care of our neighbour. My mother was hesitant initially, but when the lady insisted, she relented. Our house was surrounded by a wild growth of shrubs, plants and tall grasses. The floors looked like they hadn't been cleaned for years (which probably was the case). The walls were in desperate need of a paint job and in fact, some parts of the walls had completely collapsed too. All these entailed extensive repair work. The rooms had not been ventilated for the last two years. The rooms smelt of wet mud and of rodents' and pests' infestation.

My mother stopped in front of the homestead and as she stared at the house, she had a queer feeling...a presentiment bogged her. She asked her children to stay back and she herself moved towards the house. She then clapped her hands several times and spoke out loud, 'Snake gods, Rodent gods and Pest gods, I've come back to live here with my children. You have lived here in our absence. I beg of you, please, move away and allow us to renovate the house.' She went around the homestead, undaunted, clapping and silently praying, repeating the same words. Strangely enough, we didn't see any snakes on the homestead since that day. It worked like a miracle. Very soon, we all got busy renovating the house.

We slogged for the next fifteen days: thoroughly trimming the overgrown bushes and shrubs in the frontage and the backyard, pasting the walls and the floors of the house with thick layers of mud, closing the holes on the walls with fresh mud dough and repairing the roof by covering it with fresh thatch. The kitchen and the porches were also renovated. The holes in the wooden doors and windows were sealed with cut-to-size pieces of mosquito nets and pasted with mud and cow dung dough. The frontage and the backyard were fenced with bamboo strips sewn into mats and thick bamboo posts to prevent wandering snakes from slithering in. Luckily, Grandfather sent two labourers to help us out.

In two weeks' time, we were all set. My mother made the house a home with her touch.

One day, an elderly woman passing by the house came up to Mother, looked at her from tip to toe and said, 'Oh, you must be Nilima! I'm seeing you after so many years. So you have come to live here, right?'

Before my mother could say anything, the lady walked into our house.

'Oh, I see how pleasantly and comfortably you have settled down here, the house now looks cozy. You have a blessed pair of hands on you and a gang of such nice children too. Had you had a bowlful of good luck, you would have a dainty palace for a house, right?' the woman seemed so spiteful that it made us very uncomfortable, especially Mother.

She knew that time and fortune were not on her side. If this woman was my age or younger, I would have put her in her place, my mother thought to herself. But instead, she thanked her with utmost politeness for coming over to check on her and bent down to touch her feet.

A new morning dawned; there was light in the room when my mother woke up. She sat up, rubbing her eyes to wipe away the lingering traces of slumber. She drew in a deep breath, stretched her arms up as if gathering her strength for a long day ahead.

She then set out with a small pot hanging from the hook of her fingers in one hand and clutching an earthen pitcher under her arm to the field.

She found many women on the street and she followed them. The women chewed on a special kind of green stick which grew in abundance in the wild. They carried large pitchers under their arms for fetching water for their homes and an empty small pot in the hook of their fingers. Some even had a head-load of clothes to be washed at the river bank. She noted that life hadn't changed in the village ever since she had left the village twenty years ago. She was used to this life when she had come to that house as a daughter-in-law.

First, the women went to the river bank and offloaded the things that they carried. Then, they filled their small pots with water from the river and went into the forest to collect dry twigs and dry leaves. Some would even look for edible tubers and drumsticks. The forest was used by the villagers for open defecation too.

Like the other women in the village, Mother too went to the

river bank in the morning. She usually avoided the spots that were frequented by others. She would travel some extra distance along the bank to find a lonely spot where the water was shallow, where it almost stagnated into a shallow pool. These places usually had an abundant growth of edible leafy plants such as drumsticks. On some days, she was lucky enough to catch some tiny freshwater fish as well.

She carried a small pot and an empty pitcher on her head. She would first go to the river bank, deposit the pitcher on the bank and then proceed to the nearby forest along with the small pot with water in it. Then, she would collect green twigs and dry sticks and leaves. While the green twigs were used for brushing teeth, the dry sticks served as fuel for the kitchen hearth.

She had to intermittently straighten her body and stand straight for some time to give her muscles and back a little rest. When she had collected enough for the day, she would take her bath in the river.

She encouraged us to keep reading the textbooks and working on the workbooks that we carried with us from Jamshedpur till she managed to put us in formal schools. Although she herself did not have much formal education, she had great appreciation for education and intellectual development in growing children. She hoped to have enough money soon to put us in the village primary school.

When bad times befall someone, the whole world shuns that person. This revelation came quite early to us. One day, Mother went to Grandfather to discuss the finances. Grandfather gave her the details. He had invested ₹10,000 in his moneylending business. The money was advanced to his tenant farmer, Rama Gouda.

For Mother that was a godsend, as that meant two square meals a day. But her happiness was only short-lived. Her father narrated the application of the balance sum thus: 'Anadi had taken a loan of ₹5,000 from me. He had further taken a loan of ₹5,000 from his brother-in-law. A loan is a loan and has to be recovered from the concerned loanee's heir. So I have appropriated ₹10,000 towards the recovery of the loans.'

Mother was taken aback; she stared at Grandfather. 'I didn't have the vaguest idea ...' she blurted, flaring her nostrils.

'Business is business, my child; money loaned has to be recovered,' Grandfather explained apologetically.

'But...' she chose not to proceed further in the conversation.

She remembered her grandmother's words: 'When poverty strikes, love flies out of the window.' How right she was!

She felt the last ounce of her strength to fight for survival thinning away. She was always transparent and open about her feelings. She bit her lips and turned red. She was torn between her loyalty to her father and her bitter disappointment at his hurtful business prudence.

'I'm thus left with a balance of only ₹5,000, which I suggest you save for your eldest daughter's marriage,' Grandfather advised.

She shrugged and smiled tightly as the impending fear of the future and how she would manage the family gripped her. When she left Jamshedpur, she had a little over ₹100 with her. After paying for the bus fare and porterage, she was left with only ₹60. We did not even know when Mantoo would be getting his paycheck so that he could send some money home.

We survived on wild leafy greens for a while which she collected every day from the river bank. However, she chose not to approach Grandfather for help nor did he offer any.

Being a widow and the daughter of an affluent person, she couldn't step out of her house to do a menial job in other people's houses. However, she soon realized that she had hit rock bottom—that the only way from there was the way up. She braced herself for a fight. She decided to work in the neighbourhood.

She confided in her benignant neighbour about her situation and she was able to arrange work for her in the neighbourhood. Thus, my mother engaged in winnowing, food processing and grinding of spices in the affluent households in the neighbourhood. People didn't pay well in the countryside. Moreover, wages were paid only in kind. She got some broken rice which was enough to prepare rice gruel along with some boiled wild spinach or drumstick leaves for lunch and supper.

The work was not regular. When there was no work, we had to starve.

Our malevolent neighbour was a Brahmin lady. She adored me and called me Raja Kumar, meaning prince. One day, she called me to her house and fed me a sumptuous meal. When Mother found out about that, she was glad and unhappy at the same time; glad because I had had a sumptuous meal, sad because she was unable to feed her children even one proper meal a day. In fact, we were going through such a crisis at that time that we did not have enough oil for the two earthen lamps that we had. To save on oil, Mother would use very slim wicks made of cotton rags which only gave a slender flame. She saw to it that the children hit their beds early in the evening so that she could blow out the lamps.

One day, Mother received a strange proposal from a woman in the neighbourhood. The woman's sister was married to a doctor who was practising in the Raghunathpur dispensary. The doctor was looking for a helping hand for his wife. The woman proposed that Mother send her eight-year-old daughter, Trupti, to work in the doctor's house. We were assured that Trupti would get four meals a day and good healthcare and that apart, she would be allowed to pursue her studies at Raghunathpur. Mother was free to visit her any time. Poverty clouded my mother's perspective and she decided to send Trupti to the doctor's house.

The news reached Mantoo and he turned wild. He knew that in the village, people were like hawks, always looking for opportunities to exploit destitute children, giving them false hopes of good food and a roof above their head. He wrote a note to Mother to immediately bring her back and she was left with no choice but to give in.

Mantoo's board examination results were out in the third week of June. He was anxiously waiting for the results. We knew how difficult it was, then, for him to focus on his studies. Those days, the students preparing for their first major examination required counselling and constant attention. The poor financial condition of our family during his senior years at school ate into our parents' time. Moreover, Father's death brought in the absolute financial crisis; all that completely deranged his concentration on studies. He sat for the examination only on the insistence of Mother. So it was but natural for him to be anxious about his results. On the day of the results, he almost dragged himself to the centre. But to his utter surprise, he passed in first division. He couldn't believe his own eyes when he found his name in the first-division list. He looked up his name and roll number on the result sheet again and again just to make sure that he had read it right. His joy was boundless. He knew he owed his success to his mother, who always bolstered his confidence. Wish Mother was here with me to share this joy, he thought to himself.

He walked away from the crowd thronging the notice board and chose a quiet corner to mull over his past struggles, Father's untimely death and how Mother stood by him through thick and thin. His heart was filled with gratitude towards his mother.

What now? He wondered. There was no question of him continuing his studies further as he had to support the family.

'Mantoo.' He heard someone calling out his name from behind, 'Is everything alright with you?'

He turned to see who it was. It was Ganesh Mahapatra, his mathematics teacher. He immediately stood up and touched his teacher's feet and sought his blessings.

'How was your result? First division, I'm sure,' Mr Mahapatra queried.

'Sir, I've passed in first division, but couldn't manage a good percentage. I'm a little sad about that.'

'Congratulations, dear, I knew you would make it. I have heard of your father's accidental demise and I can understand what you have gone through these past couple of years. So what's your plan now?'

Mantoo's jubilant face suddenly turned gloomy, like a blotch of dark cloud covering the bright sun. After a brief pause, he said, 'I need to get a job. I have six siblings and Mother to look after. There is not a penny in the house. Mother, with the rest of my brothers and sisters, has moved to the village. I am already doing a salesman's job in a book shop apart from distributing newspapers early in the morning.'

Mr Mahapatra became thoughtful. After a while, he asked Mantoo to see him at his home the following Sunday.

Mantoo took the next Sunday off to meet Mr Mahapatra. When Mantoo reached Mahapatra's house, he was teaching a group of children in the first room of his house. He greeted his teacher by bowing down and touching his feet. Mahapatra was a very popular mathematics teacher.

'Mantoo, I am so glad you came. Come on in.' Mr Mahapatra got up from where he sat and ushered Mantoo to another room, where two girls were studying. 'They are my twin daughters. They are in Class IX. I am unable to guide them. I don't have time. Will you take the responsibility of teaching them? I will pay you.'

Mantoo hesitated. He did not have any experience at teaching. Teaching my teacher's daughters, he shuddered. 'I am...erm... I have no experience at teaching, sir.'

'Oh, don't worry about that. I know you can do much better than anybody else. I trust you. I shall pay as you would want. Now don't say no. You can start tomorrow.' Mantoo couldn't refuse the offer.

After taking up the teaching job, Mantoo's daily routine changed. He would wake up at 5 a.m., have his bath and finish his breakfast by 5.30 a.m., pick up newspapers from the distributor by 6 a.m., finish distributing them by 7 a.m. and reach Mahapatra's house by 7.30 a.m. He tutored his students up to 8.30 a.m. By 9.30 a.m., he would reach the bookshop and stay there till 5.30 p.m. Then he would again go to tutor till 8.30 p.m. He usually had his lunch at the bookshop. By the time he returned in the evening, he was usually too tired to cook for himself or his landlord, as was the arrangement. But the person was understanding and suggested that Mantoo drop his job of delivering newspapers. Mantoo found it to be a logical suggestion and followed it.

Mr Mahapatra knew my brother very well. He was aware of our family's financial condition. He advised Mantoo to study privately for his graduation while working as a tutor.

My brother did well as a private tutor and his efforts paid off when his students fared well in their exams. Mr Mahapatra was hard pressed for time. He ran two tuition batches in the morning and two in the evening. Not that he was greedy, but his popularity drew pupils for private tuition. Being a nice and benignant soul, he couldn't say no to any of them. He offered my brother the job of teaching one of the batches so that he remained in touch with academics and was paid for that too. So it was a win-win situation for Mantoo.

Thus my brother became a full-time private tutor at a tender age and that put him on better stead financially. Now he was able to send more money home. He gave up his salesman job at the bookstore so that he could focus on his private studies for graduation and prepare for the tutorial classes at Mr Mahapatra's house.

But in his heart, my brother missed Mother. He craved to visit the village and meet Mother, but since the academic session had already started, he couldn't take time off the tutorials; he had to postpone his visit. He decided to take time off from his tutorial assignments during Durga Puja holidays instead.

By this time, it was almost two months since we shifted to the village. Mother's kitty of ₹60 was long since spent. We continued to live on rice gruels and wild spinach. The days we didn't have rice gruel, we satiated our hunger with just wild spinach or drumsticks. Breakfast was a luxury. Our clothes were dirty and tattered. Mother had only one saree. She didn't have another saree to change after taking her bath at the river bank. She would walk home with the wet saree on and a load of the day's harvests on her head.

She was happy when she got the first remittance from Mantoo in August end that year. She put her second son, ten-year-old Annirudhha, and seven-year-old daughter, Tapu in the village primary school. Annirudhha was in Class IV and Trupti (Tapu) was in Class I. There was a letter from my brother along with the first remittance. She asked Annirudhha to read it out to her. It mentioned about his success in the XIth board examination. The letter also mentioned that he had given up his newspaper job and the salesman's job and that he had become a full-time tutor. The letter further narrated how he was helped by his teacher, Mr Mahapatra.

Mother's eyes were misty. She felt proud of her son, who was left to fend for himself at such a tender age. She tightly held the letter to her chest, her eyes teary.

Mantoo's remittances came in irregularly, as he had to wait for someone travelling to the village to send the money. The money he sent wasn't enough though. After all, ours was a big family. Besides, it was monsoon and the house demanded regular maintenance. However, the remittances did ease out Mother's worries to some extent.

Annirudhha's and Tapu's first day in school was not very pleasant. The school was not at all like the one they attended in Jamshedpur. It was no match. It was lenient, the teachers were a little slow and the students were rowdier. They could not make any friends on the first day. Throughout the day, they did not speak to anyone. Annirudhha chose the first row to sit. He stared at the blackboard and waited for the day to end.

During one of his visits to the village, my father had fixed our eldest sister's marriage in the presence of my grandfather and had assured the parents of the groom, on their insistence of course, for solemnizing the marriage at an early date, a fact which Father shared with my mother later. The groom's family was from the same village and was known very well to my father and my grandfather.

One afternoon in September that year, Grandfather visited our house. He informed my mother that the groom's side insisted on solemnizing the marriage. My mother was reluctant, as in Hindu tradition, the death of a family member is mourned for one year and no function especially marriage is solemnized during this period. Moreover, my sister was preparing for the Certified Trained Teacher programme privately and marriage at that juncture would mean an end to her academic career.

'Look, Nilima,' said my grandfather, trying to convince Mother, 'this alliance has been fixed by Anadi. Now that he is gone, his commitment is to be respected and acted upon. Moreover, our society hasn't evolved so much as to accept a highly educated girl as a prospective bride. You're a widow. Who would like to have a relation with a widow? I'm afraid you may not get a marriage proposal again for your daughter if you skip this alliance. And you know what a burden and embarrassment it will be to have an unmarried girl in your house.'

Mother contemplated over the subject for days and finally it was decided to solemnize the marriage soon after Dussehra, so that Mantoo could attend the wedding. When the news reached my eldest sister, she was crestfallen. She was afraid she wouldn't be able to continue with her studies if she was married and her dream of becoming self-dependent would be squashed. She cursed her life as a girl.

One day, while asleep in Mother's lap, all of a sudden, my eldest sister began mumbling, 'Mother! ... Mother! ... Mother!' She woke up with a jerk.

'Dreams are dreams. Just let go!' My mother consoled her as she took her in her embrace and began caressing her hair.

'Mother! Oh, Mother, how could you think of getting me married and sending me off to a stranger's house especially at a time when I have just begun to know you as a mother and when I have just begun to enjoy the bliss of motherly love? I have not yet forgotten that last meal I had with Father in Cuttack before we travelled to Kalarabanka. The scene still haunts me. Please, don't send me off so early; please don't deprive me of your love and affection so early, please.' She was separated from her parents and started living in the village when she was just a year old. The memories of this separation haunted her at the subconscious level and the thought of leaving behind her own family and especially her dear mother took a toll on her. She felt helpless.

'How can I stop all this from happening, dear? You know the situation better than anyone else. Please don't get emotional about it. You are breaking my heart. You are already nineteen, my dear. This is the ideal time for you to get married and you won't get a better match than this. And that was your father's last wish. What if you never get married? I can't have that on my conscience.'

A date in November that year, 1969, was scheduled for the wedding and Mantoo was informed beforehand, so that he could schedule a trip to the village around that time.

Since my mother was a widow, she did not need her gold ornaments. Even during grueling times, my parents did not sell off their jewellery. The State Bank of India had opened a new branch at Raghunathpur. For the wedding, with the help of Grandfather, Mother was able to pledge a part of her ornaments with the bank and avail a loan of ₹5,000 while the remaining ornaments were exchanged in the goldsmith's shop for fresh ones.

After my eldest sister's wedding, Annirudhha started living with our grandfather. After the death of our grandmother, Grandfather had grown quite lonely. Besides, he was old too. Soon, it was time for Annirudhha to pursue his further studies. The high school was in

Raghunathpur, almost nine kilometers away from the village. Many of the boys and girls in the village couldn't continue their studies beyond primary school because they couldn't go to Raghunathpur. There was no proper road to Raghunathpur. One had to go through the village forest and moors and cross the river Paika. That was tough for a twelve-year old boy who was not used to the hard village life.

When Mantoo had come to the village to attend his elder sister's wedding, he realized Annirudhha's plight. Both my mother and Mantoo conferred on the matter of Annirudhha's education and they decided that Annirudhha should go to Jamshedpur for his further studies. When Annirudhha moved in with Mantoo, they decided to take up another accommodation near Mr Mahapatra's house, so that he could comfortably conduct his tutorial classes from there. Besides, he did not want to overstay his welcome at his previous landowner's house.

With the eldest daughter married off, Mother started worrying about her second daughter, Trupti's wedding. She was fifteen then. She did not have enough money for a fancy wedding ceremony. If she were to be married, it had to be by a special provision called Tola-Kanya-Vivaha, in which the girl is simply sent off to the groom's house without a formal ceremony; it was like gifting the girl. Such a system was in practice in poor households and was socially approved too.

Fortunately, Mother received one such marriage alliance through Grandfather from a respectable Bengali family in Cuttack. The groom worked in a bucket-making factory in Cuttack, so he made a modest income. A day was scheduled for the groom's parents to come and see the girl. However, there was one problem. My sister did not have a decent saree to wear that day. My mother asked her neighbours to lend them a saree for a day, but in vain. Fortunately, the family accepted my sister as she was and in a year's time, she was married off too.

Mantoo got into service with the Tata Company in 1972, the year he turned twenty. He was appointed as a time-keeper. He should have got the job when he was eighteen, but his application for a job in the company took a couple of years to get processed.

When the news of Mantoo getting the job reached my mother, she felt as if a great load was taken off her frazzled shoulders. She shut her eyes as though trying to get a grip on herself. The memories of her husband came flooding back, every bit of it, from their first meeting to when he left this earth for his heavenly abode. She could see his face vividly. His untimely death was an appalling blow, shattering her world. She had to be brave for her children and she could finally see a silver lining. Mantoo's new job rekindled many hopes in us and Mother. Despite her altercation with Grandfather about the money incident, he was the first person Mother always went to during good times and bad. So, when she told Grandfather about Mantoo's new job, he blessed him from the bottom of his heart.

Back in Jamshedpur, Mantoo was going steady with his job at Tata Company. He was also doing his private tutorial job during off-duty hours. He sent money to his mother through fellow villagers as and when they visited the village. He managed with half of his earnings at Jamshedpur while remitting the other half to our family.

Though the pangs of hunger partially eased out, a full square meal a day was still a distant dream for us. Very little money was left after paying the interest on the gold loan that my mother had availed from the bank at the time of our eldest sister's wedding and also house renovation. She did not lose any opportunity to pick up odd jobs and enterprises now and then to augment the allowance that she received from Mantoo.

In the meanwhile, our eldest sister was in the family way and we were all elated on hearing the news. Tapu was sent off to her house as a helping hand. Moreover, our eldest sister would help Tapu with her studies.

However, one day, Mother found out that Tapu was being ill-treated at our eldest sister's place. Mother was looking for an opportunity to get Tapu back home. One day when Mantoo visited the village, she asked him to fetch Trupti back from his eldest sister's house and take her to Jamshedpur, so that she could pursue her studies better.

Tapu was eleven years old then and in Class VI. In a year's time, she was to complete her primary schooling and go out for her higher studies, the chances of which were rather bleak in the village. She was a good student and so it was decided that Tapu should also go and stay with Mantoo and Annirudhha in Jamshedpur and pursue her further studies there.

Five years had come to pass, but Rama Gauda did not show up nor did he pay the interest on the principal amount. Mother was due to receive six bags (a little over 400 kgs) of paddy from him towards the interest on the money lent to him. October and November were the harvesting months. Mother eagerly awaited every harvest and kept reminding Grandfather about Gauda's indifference.

Several more months passed without any news from Gauda or Grandfather. She finally decided to take on Gauda on her own without depending on Grandfather. She rushed to Gauda's house, but he was not home. She ascertained from his neighbour that he was in his field tending to a brick kiln. She pussyfooted to the field and startled him. 'Rama Gauda, you have played enough, I am through with your games. I am here to get back my money back and all interest till date. I shall not budge an inch without getting them, failing which I shall make your life miserable.'

Sensing the gravity of the situation, Gauda fell at her feet and prayed for a few more days' time, assuring her that when the bricks were ready, he would repay the loan with interest in the form of bricks. He promised to send two cartloads of bricks to her homestead to cover a part of the interest.

When the carts of bricks finally arrived, my mother felt happy and proud because it was nothing short of an achievement. The sight of the stack of bricks at her homestead reminded her of how Father always longed to renovate the house. He often visualized a small and cozy house with a boundary wall and an arched gate. That was the only property he had that he could call his own. Even she had many sentiments attached to the house—the house where she had come as a bride. She wanted her children to be proud of their ancestral house and accept it for whatever it was. She also believed that a proper house would provide her children with confidence and pride. She foresaw that a proper house would draw her children to the homestead and they would stay connected with the village, with their roots.

For many months thereafter there was no word from Rama Gauda. That compelled Mother to accost him once again for the return of the principal amount loaned. This time, she found him loading his brick kiln. Mother struck a deal with Gauda for the supply of bricks, as she would need them for renovation of the house. She warned him of dire consequences if he refused the deal.

She started saving the monthly allowance Mantoo sent her to buy cement and associated aggregates. She didn't have much ground for accommodating fresh stacks of bricks and so needed to clear the space for more bricks. She had to use all the bricks that were presently stacked on the homestead as the next batch of bricks would be out in a couple of months' time. So she needed to use up the existing stock of bricks. She planned to first build the boundary wall. Using the available bricks, she was able to put the foundation of the boundary wall.

The following month, Mantoo visited the village and was surprised to see the boundary wall. Those days, even the rich and the influential people didn't wish to construct boundary walls around their homesteads. It was considered an unnecessary expense. Mother narrated her tiff with Gauda to Mantoo and the arrangement arrived at.

'Look, Mantoo, your grandfather had demarcated the boundary by surrounding the homestead with bamboo fence and bamboo posts.

I replaced them when we came here. I need to protect my in-laws' property, which they managed to get after a protracted struggle. A brick-mortar boundary wall was necessary to protect the homestead from any encroachment in the future. Moreover, I stay here with your young brothers and sisters under a constant threat of snakes entering this premises.'

'Mother, I shall never meet in my life a person like you, a person with such energy and determination, but I feel sad that you and the kids had to starve for the sake of the house.' Mantoo let his mother have her way because he knew that once she had made up her mind, she would stretch to any extent to accomplish it.

8

SOMETHING ISN'T RIGHT

'Mother, can I get something to eat? I am very hungry!' Sukuta begged his mother. But Nilimarani was fast asleep. She was exhausted from working all morning and noon. Itina too was asleep by her side. Finishing her morning routine, there was nothing much to do that day. She combed her hair and tied it in a neat bun and reclined on the wall of her room. That is when she started brooding over her situation.

This was not the only time she was reflective. There were times when she brooded for hours. It became her second nature. Mother stayed up many nights wondering what the future had in store for her family. She had dark circles around her eyes from lack of sleep. The change that she was looking forward to was still out of her sight, but she had a gut feeling that fate was not going to be unkind forever. And thus reflecting about the past, the present and the future, Mother fell asleep without even realizing.

Her intuitive feelings were not entirely wrong. Her life and ours went through a potent energetic shift—an extraordinary time of change that had begun the moment Father met with the tragic accident. It was beyond any one to understand the intrigues of life and she was no exception. However, the onset of unprecedented obstacles, challenges and hardship had a definite purpose which was woven into the fabric of her life by Providence. The 'chaos' that was the most significant part of her life was perhaps all part of a magnificent shift—and she prayed that in the midst of this chaos, Providence would present some opportunity for them, an opportunity for growth. The trying times pushed us out of our comfort zones. We grew bolder and more daring, ready to undertake any challenge. Mother was beginning to see a transformation in the way we viewed life.

She taught us not to take anything for granted. We learned to live with minimalistic needs and we lived in the present. If we had food, we ate; if we didn't, we didn't crib. We learned to accept life as it unfolded each day. It didn't matter if we were criticized or ridiculed. We simply went on doing our work and rallied around our mother. Life taught us to be humble, and to love and respect others. And with those values, we moved on in life.

It was late in the afternoon. The sun was setting in the western horizon. The faint sunlight seeped into the room through the window. Sukuta felt the warmth of the sun on his skin. He was back from school. He studied in a high school in Raghunathpur. The distance to the school was about five miles and he commuted on foot. He was tired. His legs were aching. He was famished.

'Mother, I am hungry.'

Nilimarani was fast asleep with her daughter, Itina (Iti). Sukuta's call did not wake her up.

He called again, 'Mother, can I get something to eat? I'm hungry!'

This time she heard his call. Sleepily, she rubbed her eyes and looked at Sukuta for a while before she recalibrated herself with the situation. 'Go to the kitchen, Sukuta. I have kept some rice gruel for you. You may have it all.' Sukuta gave her a smile and went into the kitchen. After finishing his lunch, he came back into the bedroom. 'Mother, I am going to the kitchen garden,' he said, stepping out.

My mother's gaze followed the receding steps of her son. When his figure was no longer visible, she flung herself onto the mat and closed her eyes. She remained that way for a long time before she woke up again. Poverty has its sunny side too. It gives us the satisfaction of working with our head and our heart. It is a blessing in disguise, she reflected. Her little Sukuta was very laborious. He was mature beyond his years. When most of the boys his age whiled away their time playing in the fields, Sukuta would go straight to the kitchen garden and tend to the vegetables. He would also go to the river and fetch water in pitchers for drinking and water for the plants. That was part of his daily routine. With those thoughts, she drifted into a flashback mode. 'Mother, can I have something to eat? I am very hungry!' she heard Sukuta say. It brought back some heart-rending memories.

'Mother, can I have something to eat? I am hungry!'

It was 1970...a late morning in the month of September and Sukuta was seven then. He had just come home after his usual morning outing in the village, playing with his friends. He picked up a few friends on his way home. He loved to play and his friends always gave him company. They assembled at the end of the village, close to the forest, every morning and evening, where there was an expanse of open space that served as their playground.

Mother was sleeping with Itina. My sister Anupama was out in the forest, from where she had gone to the riverbank for her ablutions. Upon returning from the river, she swept the front and rear porches of the house and the kitchen. She even did the dishes. Annirudhha and Trupti were at school. After some time, Mother woke up and left home on her usual morning routine. When she was back home and was about to cook lunch, she realized that there was not a grain left in the house. She prepared rice gruel with whatever stock of broken rice was left over from the previous day.

'Mother, can I have something to eat? I am very hungry!' Sukuta asked.

She looked at his face. She was full of remorse. 'No!' she said, shaking her head.

But the seven-year-old Sukuta was not disappointed at all. His countenance remained unfazed. Life has always been like that for him. He sat down by his mother's side. She felt miserable having to say no to him. Her stress level rose and her empty stomach only added to her misery. She heard her stomach roar and she felt nausea sweeping over her. She closed her eyes and took several deep breaths and tried to steady herself. After a while, she began to feel better again. She realized that there was some leftover rice gruel from the previous evening. Annirudhha and Trupti had eaten a small portion of the gruel before leaving for school. Some of it was still left in the earthen bowl. She asked Sukuta to go into the kitchen and look up.

'There is a bowl in the kitchen with some rice gruel in it, did you find?' Mother shouted from her room.

'It's right here, yes, there is something here in the pot, can I have it, Mother?

'Yes, but spare some for your younger sister too!'

Sukuta left a few morsels of gruel for his sister. He returned to the bedroom. His mother was still lying in the mat with her eyes closed. After returning from the river bank, she always went out into the neighbourhood for work.

'Mother, are you alright?' Sukuta inquired.

'Yes. I am simply resting a bit. I am perfectly alright. My dear little son, don't get worked up. I am going to work in a while and will be back soon. Keep guard of the house and take care of your little sister.'

He stretched his tender arms and rushed towards his mother, intending to give her a hug, which he did very often. An emotionally charged Mother pulled Sukuta and held him in a tight embrace. He felt the scars in her palm, the tell-tale signs of hardship and endurance. 'Where is it you want to go, Mother? Should I come with you? Maybe I can help you in your work,' said Sukuta. 'And what happened to your hands?'

'It's nothing. And now look, you will not come with me but stay here with your little sister. Don't go anywhere leaving her alone!'

'It's alright, Mother. I only thought I could be of some help!'

Oh my child...oh my child!' she kissed Sukuta's forehead in a melancholy manner and stroked his cheeks with her scarred palms. Sukuta quickly took hold of his mother's hands and began intently looking at them. He opened his mouth to speak but quickly pursed his lips and began caressing her palms. Mother gently pulled her hands away from him. He looked disappointed.

'I don't think you'll ever like to take a morsel of food from these wretched palms, Sukuta.'

'Mother, I love it when you feed me with your hands,' Sukuta said, clutching onto his mother's saree.

'You had the last handful of rice gruel and now there is not a grain left in the house. Your brother and sister will be home soon. I have to go find something for lunch and supper.' Mother got up, arranged her saree, tidied her hair into a low bun and marched out through the front door.

Sukuta was sad seeing his mother go out. He was sad that his mother had to go out to work even when she wasn't feeling well. Sukuta followed his mother for a while till she was no longer visible. Sukuta imagined himself sitting beside her and sharing rice gruel with her that he had left in the pot. I should have shared the food with Mother too, he thought to himself.

Sukuta walked into the kitchen and returned with the bowl that had the leftover rice gruel. He shut the door behind him and walked to where his sister was asleep. He woke her up. He took the bowl and peeked into it. There was still a handful of the rice gruel in it. He fed it to his sister. He longed to have some of the food, but chose to feed his sister instead.

Sukuta proceeded to keep the pot back in the kitchen. When he neared the front door, he suddenly realized that the door was wide open and he flinched. Why is the door open? he wondered. He stood there at the threshold for some time and then started walking down to the kitchen at the end of the porch. He could feel strong winds ruffling his hair. He looked skyward; it was dark. The coconut treetops were twisting and swaying. He strained his gaze towards the pathway and saw his mother approaching. He rushed back into the room and hollered, 'See, Mother's come, Mother's come.' Annirudhha and

Anupama, who were back from school by then, looked at him and then all of them rushed to the door to welcome her. But they didn't see anybody there. 'You must have had a dream!' Annirudhha quipped. They all sat there on the porch. Hours passed, but there was no sign of Mother's coming. 'Sukuta was perhaps mistaken,' Annirudhha told Anupama and both smiled. 'Why, what's your anxiety, my dear sweet, little brother?' Anupama asked Sukuta. She wondered if Sukuta was intensely yearning for his mother to be home for food. 'Come inside, dear, Mother will be back anytime soon!' she coaxed Sukuta.

'No. She was here, I'm sure. I think she went off somewhere else.' He walked up to the gate. The lightning and the sun hiding behind the clouds were the only source of brightness that day. The sound of the wind turned into a roar. Sukuta kept looking in the direction where he had caught a glance of his mother. A man was passing by. When he saw the boy out in the open during the approaching storm, he said, 'Boy, off you trot back into your house. It is going to storm.'

'I am not going to trot off.' He resolved. 'I am going to wait here till Mother returns.' He stood there near the fence, staring at the road. He saw a boy approaching. He was eating a banana. In his left hand, he was holding another banana. He was clearly enjoying the banana; he was biting it, sometimes licking it and at other times, nibbling it, bit by bit. Sukuta watched the boy and the way he was relishing it.. Sukuta began drooling. Dragging his feet, he faltered back to the room where Annirudhha and Anupama were sleeping and flung himself on the mat beside Anupama.

After what seemed to be an hour or so, Sukuta felt his mother's fingers stroking his hair. He woke up with a jerk. Yes, she was back.

'It's okay, Mother, you're okay, you're not hurt. You're not, are you?' He threw himself on his mother and hugged her tight.

'Yes, dear, I'm perfectly okay.'

'Please don't go out now, Mother!' Sukuta pleaded, holding the free end of her saree. He felt a bulge wrapped around the end of the saree. He touched it, trying to feel and guess the contents.

'There must be something for us in that!' he queried, running his hand over the bulge. A smile spread across Mother's lips. Sukuta opened the knot of the saree.

'Ah, some broken rice,' he exclaimed.

'Yes, darling, for you and your brothers and sisters to share.'

'No, Mother, we all shall share, including you.'

'Let me prepare some gruel for you all,' she said, rising and lumbering to the kitchen. As the gruel was simmering, Mother looked out of the window and gazed at the sky. She saw a dull orange glow on the western horizon. Dark clouds covered the sky. A strong wind had begun to blow. She realized it could rain anytime. There might be a storm even, she thought to herself. Storms were not uncommon in these part of the country because of its proximity to the Bay of Bengal.

The wind grew stronger and stronger. The dark clouds looming in the sky got thicker and darker. The trees, small and big, began to sway vigorously. The dry branches and ripe fruits began falling off the trees.

Mother feared that the strong winds would blow away the roof of our house, but she did not know how to prevent that from happening. So all she could do was pray. The sound of the dropping coconuts and the crashing sound of the falling fronds rose Sukuta's curiosity. He came out and sat on the porch. He seemed to enjoy the feel of the strong wind. In a couple of hours, the storm grew stronger, rather fierce. The wind made a whistling sound as it made its way through the foliage. The thatch roof creaked. A creepy feeling sneaked into their hearts. He didn't stir from where he sat. Rain hit the earth with such force that it nearly dug the earth. Streams of water began flowing on the road in the front of the house. Nothing beyond a distance of ten feet was visible. He didn't move, even when the slanting rain lashed his body. The rain seemed vengeful. The whole village was deserted. Not a soul was to be seen. The trees swayed in a frenzy. Sukuta lurched forward and picked up the fallen coconuts and stacked them on the porch. Suddenly, it occurred to him that there were a lot of coconut trees on the canal embankment and he should be able to get more of those fallen coconuts there.

Sukuta was mature for his age. He was quick to figure out how things worked. He was daring and inquisitive. He loved exploring on his own. He loved visiting his neighbours and interacting with them. Our neighbour, an elderly lady, had a soft spot for him and always invited him over. They would often chat and she was kind enough to feed him a sumptuous meal at times. My mother was grateful for that. *There were kind and caring people in the world after all.* Sukuta was quite popular with the village kids too. There was something about him that drew people towards him. 'Sukuta has come, let's play,' the children would shout and come running towards him. A game of catch-catch and hide-and-seek were their favourite pastimes. They would play till their bones creaked and body ached.

That evening, Sukuta found himself gripped by a strange curiosity. He took several deep breaths. He tried to restrain himself from the urge to venture out into the open. He took a short walk towards the fence. The rain lashed at him. He covered his face but got drenched. The wind and the rain were chilly and he had goosebumps all over his body, but he was not one to be daunted. He stood there, defiant against the raging storm. He opened his palms and stretched them forward. A coconut frond fell a little distance away and the sound startled him. He looked up. Suddenly, he heard a loud thud from behind; a whole bunch of coconuts had fallen from a tree. He could wait no more. He gave a fleeting glance at the house behind him and quietly slipped out onto the street without letting anyone know. He walked a few careful steps and then sprinted towards the canal that passed by the fringe of the village. He had a plan. He would collect the fallen coconuts along the embankment and request his mother to sell them off. When he reached the canal, dripping wet, he found that the embankment was indeed littered with fallen fronds and coconuts. With his tender hands, he began collecting the fallen coconuts, fronds and other parts of the trees. Then he ran back home to dump them, and came back for more.

Nobody saw him—nobody. Not even a ghost or a stray dog was on the embankment or on the streets. The villagers had locked themselves inside their huts and cottages. The wind lashed at him. The trees hung their heads, as if in despair. Sukuta could hear the windows of some of the houses slam open and shut. The leaves were heavy, the branches heavier, some cracked and fell onto the ground as he tried to lift them. But nothing could stop Sukuta in this dangerous mission.

On a hunch, Mother woke up. She sat up, peeked through the window and realized that a nasty and fearsome storm was raging outside. The wind and rain made her vision hazy and she couldn't see very far. All she could see was the mad swaying, twisting, curving, rising and falling rain. She scanned the room. Sukuta was not there. Her heart slumped. She got up with a jerk. Dashing through the middle room, then through the front one, she reached the threshold of the front door and stared at the raging storm. Sukuta was nowhere to be seen. She slumped onto the floor. She shivered violently seeing the carnage that ensued; the trees were writhing, flailing and moaning, the rain was hammering an impenetrable salvo of bullets as the clouds above spat lightning mercilessly. She pulled the free end of her saree over her head tightly. A strange fear gripped her. *Something isn't right. Something definitely isn't right.* She could no more bear Sukuta's absence. She stepped out onto the street alone. 'Sukuta! Sukuta!' she yelled at the top of her voice, confused which direction to go looking for him. 'Sukuta, Sukuta, Sukuta,' she called out again and again, but the storm drowned out her voice; it could not cut through the roar of the torrential rain, the roar of the wind and the deafening cacophony of the creaking, slashing and thud sounds of the falling coconut fronds. *Has he gone over to a friend's house? Why would he in this weather*? Suddenly, she saw a silhouette approaching in her direction. When the figure came very near, she recognized it. 'Sukuta,' she screamed, running towards him. He was pulling a couple of coconut fronds with a load of coconuts piled on top of them.

Sukuta could see his mother's bloodshot eyes; he spoke before she could say anything and quickly put forth his explanation, 'Mother, I thought it will fetch us some money if we sell these. I've made a pile on the porch already. Did you see?'

Mother was stunned. Sukuta's voice, though quiet as a breath, was fierce with determination. His calmness and honesty calmed Mother's rage. She held his hand. The wind shoved her to the right and the left, but she kept pushing through. A jagged bolt of lightning ripped the sky in half, the violent wind blew her veil off her head, the rain lashed at her skin, but she kept walking. When they reached home, she noticed the pile of coconuts and fallen coconut fronds. She was surprised at the boy's concern for the family. Her heart melted and she could neither shout at the boy nor cry. She folded her hands and silently thanked God that her boy was safe.

The night was dark and wet. Mother hadn't seen such a frightening night in her life so far. The uncertainty of the future and looming fears took her sleep away. The house shook under the impact of the heavy rain. For the third consecutive day, she lay hungry through the night. Hunger burned her insides. Sukuta insisted that they drink the coconut water, as there were plenty of coconuts, but Mother refused. 'Tomorrow we will hand these over to the villagers, as the harvest lawfully belongs to the whole village and not just us,' she declared. She waited anxiously for daybreak. As the darkness faded, the sun cuddled under a blanket of clouds. It hid and flitted out from behind the clouds. The rain had stopped by then. The stove was damp. It was time for Mother to leave her bed and get into the rut. Her body needed some sunlight too. Her legs were wobbly as she dragged herself out of bed.

The agony of poverty and hardship blinded my mother so much that many things escaped her notice. Her sixth and seventh children were growing up and they needed to have proper names. The sixth child was short and frail, so she called him Sukuta. However, he wasn't really weak. He was agile. She called her seventh child, Itina, meaning 'the end.' When we shifted to the village, Sukuta was four years old and Itina was only three months old. Presently, Sukuta was seven years and Itina was three years old. While Sukuta had a faint resemblance of Father, Itina had none.

Sukuta was very fond of his doll-like younger sister, who also enjoyed his company. When she was just a baby, she flapped her hands and legs vigorously and giggled aloud when Sukuta babysat her while Mother was away at work or was busy doing household chores. Now that Nilimarani's elder kids were gone, she spent most of her time working in the neighbourhood while Sukuta kept guard of the house and Itina.

'Mother, Mother, the school teacher got me admitted to the school today.' Sukuta came home running one day. He raised his hands; in one he held a slate and in the other, a bundle of writing chalks and waved those for his mother to see. His thrill and excitement were visible from the bounce in his step. One day, he had asked his mother why he didn't go to school like the other boys in the village and as his elder brother and sister did. His mother had explained that it was their poverty that stopped her from putting him in a school. He didn't press the matter thereafter.

This happened in the fall of 1972. Winter was just about setting in. The air was getting cooler with each passing day. During fall and winter, the children stayed indoors, tucked under straw quilts, only stepping out during the noon to bask in the sun and play with friends.

Sukuta went out to play with his friends after his mother returned home. The children were playing hide-and-seek in the field at the end of the village. The primary school was close to the field where the children played. The school was in session. Some raucous children strayed into the school intending to hide behind the school's walls. Sukuta was one of them. Hearing the commotion, the head teacher came out of his room and caught hold of Sukuta while the other kids fled.

'Hey! Hey! Hey! How dare you? What are you doing here?' The teacher asked Sukuta, pinching his cheeks.

Sukuta remained unfazed. 'Sir, we were playing hide-and-seek. I came here to hide from the other kids. It didn't occur to me that the school is in session.' His upper body was bare and sweat trickled down his head.

The teacher looked at the little boy. He was amazed at his simplicity and candid remark.

'Don't you go to school?' he asked Sukuta.

'No.'

'Why?'

'My mother says we are poor, so she can't put me in a school.'

'Do you want to study?'

'Yes, but I don't have a slate and chalk and books.'

'Come inside, son.'

The little boy meekly followed the teacher into his room. The teacher sat in his chair. He then pulled out a register and opened a new folio.

'What's your name, son?'

'Sukuta, that's the name my mother calls me by.'

'He, he... What kind of a name is that? Don't you have a proper name?'

'I don't know what you mean. I mean, what is a proper name?' Sukuta asked, scratching his head.

'What's your father's name?'

'Anadi Samanta.'

'What does he do?'

'He is d...dead. I've not seen much of him nor do I re...remember much of him,' he stuttered, lowering his head. A sudden sense of melancholy gripped him.

'Oh, I am so sad to hear that, son.' He paused for a while and then continued, 'How old are you?'

'I don't know.'

The teacher raised his brows and stared at the boy for a while without uttering a word. The boy was still unfazed. He didn't have a shirt on him, his body was dirty and hair unkempt. He wore a half-pant that desperately needed a wash. His flat belly almost touched his back. Despite all that, his solemn countenance impressed the teacher. He took a pen and began writing something in the register. Then he got up, walked to a cupboard on the wall, pulled out a slate and a few chalks. Handing over the same to Sukuta, he said: 'Here is your slate and here are your chalks. I have given you a new name. Achyuta, Achyuta Samanta. I have admitted you to our school. You will come regularly, won't you?' Sukuta nodded, beaming with happiness.

'Ask your mother to come to the school to complete the paperwork, will you?'

'Yes, sir,' Sukuta replied at once.

The new name gave him great self-esteem. Every time he uttered his new name, his eyes widened and a smile appeared on his lips. His mind was filled with the brilliance of a summer sun and the playful colours of a rainbow. He began painting more and more colours to the rainbows. Every pore in his body exuded a warm glow. The event ignited his passion for studies. It marked the beginning of a new life for Sukuta, now Achyuta Samanta. He ran to his mother, beaming with pride and his heart filled with happiness.

Sukuta alias Achyuta began going to school from the next day onwards. The school and the time spent there filled him with a sense of thrill and purpose. He was excited about everything at school. He sat in the class with unflinching diligence and listened to the teachers with rapt attention. Soon, his teachers realized that he was a quick learner. Though the class had advanced much in the lessons, in no time, he was able to catch up. His sharp wit, focus and quick comprehension of the lessons amazed his teachers. It didn't matter what he wore to school or what he ate for breakfast. Looking at the boy's interest in studies, all the teachers started taking extra care of him. He became the teachers' pet. When back home after school, he would settle down for his studies because studying after sunset was not permitted. Everything had to be finished before sunset so that the family could save on the oil for the lamps.

Mother wasn't able to leave Itina alone at home and go to work, as Sukuta left home for school early. She started taking Itina to her morning tasks. Sukuta's school got over by 11 a.m. After school hours, Achyuta began assisting his mother in her work. He would go to different households in the village and collect raw paddy and both the mother and son would parboil them in their courtyard. The villagers usually ate parboiled rice. Parboiling was a cumbersome process and most people in the village outsourced the job. Our mother saw great potential in this enterprise. Besides, during her growing-up years, she observed the process of parboiling, which was a regular activity in her house. She made all the arrangements in the courtyard for the enterprise. As wages, she received a small portion of the rice.

Nilimarani soon took a piece of land on lease from the landlady near our homestead. She and Sukuta cleared the land and tilled it using borrowed implements. They watered the field by carrying water from the river in pitchers on their heads. They tilled the land, again and again. They added cow-dung manure to the soil and in a few weeks' time, the field was ready for growing vegetable crops. Initially, they collected seeds from the zamindar's house but later, they picked up seeds from their own fields. Achyuta took the harvests to the nearby weekly market at Raghunathpur, which was a few miles away. This enterprise fetched us a little cash and met our family's needs to some extent.

Things were looking up for Mantoo too. He completed his graduation and started appearing for examinations to get a bank job. His efforts paid off and he received an appointment letter from a bank. It took him some time to get relieved from the Tata Company job, but he eventually joined the bank. The pay was better than what he was getting at the Tata Company. As a child, he had once asked Father why he wasn't taking a transfer to the village. Father had answered that he was working in a company that didn't have any other branch. Mantoo was therefore always on the lookout for an opportunity to relocate to his village. Banks had branches. He was disappointed that he couldn't get a transfer to Cuttack because the bank didn't have a branch there. Moreover, the bank's policy on transfers was very rigid. Not long thereafter, Mantoo's tenacity landed him a job in the Life Insurance Corporation of India and in a few years' time, he managed to get a transfer to Cuttack.

Mantoo always longed to be near his family, so his delight knew no bounds when he received his transfer order. After all, he had been living away from his family for almost eleven years.

Achyuta and Itina were in classes X and class VII respectively at that time. For Mantoo, it had become a lot easier to look after his sibling's education and grooming because of his posting in Cuttack. He usually visited the village on weekends. Tapu returned to the village while Annirudhha stayed back in Jamshedpur for his XIIth examination. Mantoo arranged for his stay with a friend of his. Tapu was in Class XI. Mantoo's coming to Cuttack brought a new lease of life to the Samanta household. Mother was happy. Her two daughters, Trupti and Anupama, were already happily settled in life with their husbands and children.

It was a great day when Mother learned that her Sukuta had passed Class Xth board examination with flying colours. There was a time when she felt she wouldn't be able to provide him with an education. Her fears were proved wrong when Sukuta took admission in the village primary school. 'Sukuta, now that you have completed Class X, what do you wish to do further? Do speak with Mantoo about your future studies when he visits the village next,' she advised.

Nilimarani wanted him to go for higher studies, like Mantoo, and even more if possible. Sukuta, however, had a different plan playing in his mind. He wanted to start an enterprise in the village to help supplement the family's income. He was always wary of the burden being shouldered solely by his eldest brother.

'Mother, I think I will stay in the village to start some enterprise and support Brother. He has been taking the burden of the family singlehandedly for all these years. I don't need to study any more. Moreover, when I go away from the village, you will be all alone. Who will look after you and the modest agricultural enterprise that we have been doing? You too are ageing. You need care and attendance. Please allow me to stay here with you.'

Nilimarani looked at him, quizzingly. She gathered herself and with a hint of sternness said, 'Hold on! That's very silly of you to think that you need to take care of me. I can stand on my own. I am not that old. I have gathered much wisdom as I travelled through life. I can take care of myself. I want you to stand on your own feet too and for that, you need to study further. Talk to Mantoo when he comes home next time.'

When Mantoo visited the village the following weekend, he firmly told Sukuta to prepare for higher studies. 'Don't worry about money. You are a good student and have managed to brave the odds and get admission into college,' Mantoo told him assertively. Achyuta heeded his brother's advice.

Achyuta went on to do his master's degree from Utkal University, Bhubaneswar. Itina too completed her Xth and shifted to Bhubaneswar, where she studied at Rama Devi Women's University.

It was a lazy autumn morning. Nilimarani sat in the front porch of her house. She was in a contemplative mood. The fluttering of the birds and the cacophony of their chirping resonated with nature's charms. The butterflies gaily hopped from one flower to another, collecting nectar. No amount of education can compare to what can be learnt from these small mysteries of life. Nilimarani's nest was empty now, the children were away from the village, living their own lives. They had grown wings. They were tied down to their own lives, but her youngest son, Achyuta, was yet to build his own nest. He had taken up the job of an acamedician in a college. He visited the village quite often.

Nilimarani looked forward to her youngest son's marriage now that Itina, too, was married. When he visited the village next, her first question was, 'When are you getting married?'

'Please don't push me into that. I have missions to accomplish and miles to go before I achieve my goals. I won't be continuing with the job for long. I want to have a meaningful existence. I want to live a giver's life.' Nilimarani heard Achyuta's words and was stunned. She had observed Achyuta very closely from a very early age. He was always fond of bringing happiness to others. He loved working hard for others' happiness. He loved sharing his earnings with needy people. Many a time, Nilimarani had spoken to him about not squandering money and to that he would say, 'Charity doesn't fall under squandering.'

She was afraid that the boy would become a total ascetic. What could be harder for a restless, ambitious boy than giving up his own dreams, plans and desires and cheerfully living for others? She knew the path he had chosen was very challenging and arduous. At times, he would feel lonely, too. She brooded over the matter. Here was the journey she didn't expect Achyuta to choose, a journey many a rich wouldn't even dare to venture into. The road to philanthropy was extremely dicey. No mother would ever approve of their child shunning worldly happiness for the sake of others. She had never in her life imposed her thoughts on her children. However, this decision was like a bolt out of the blue. She fell silent. She decided to dissuade him once again. 'Think it over. I wouldn't know much about this, nor do I make out much of this modern world's ways.'

Achyuta narrated how disturbed he was when he saw the sufferings of the poor people in the state. 'Don't you think I can help them, Mother?' he asked her.

She never doubted her children and what they were capable of achieving. The way Mantoo shouldered the responsibility of the entire family was exemplary. The way Achyuta toiled shoulder-to-shoulder with her to augment the family's income was praiseworthy. She was grateful for being blessed with such wonderful children. Achyuta was trustworthy and a man of commitment and tenacity. He wasn't sentimental, didn't say much but loved to help and that made her very happy. She knew how good, generous and soft-hearted he was.

'You have plans?' she asked, curious.

'Yes, I want to dedicate my life to the service of the poor and the backward people. I want to be a social entrepreneur and make education accessible to all.'

Nilimarani became thoughtful and worried. She looked at Achyuta's face, amazement writ large on her face. Her eyes narrowed, still trying to take in what her son had just said. She didn't know how to respond.

'How fulfilling and enriching it will be to serve others, isn't it, Mother? That has always been my dream—it excites me, it satisfies me. I am blessed to have the power of giving freely and I am grateful to you, Mother, because I've learned that from you. And now when I am ready to work towards my dream, won't you support me, Mother?' He knew his mother couldn't say no to him.

'I will.' Her whole life, she had tried to keep her children safe and now she had to put aside her softness and motherly feelings to support her son in his endeavour.

While Achyuta did get opportunities to work in the remote areas of Odisha, he had seen many talented young people making sacrifices and enduring real hardships, just like him. They were brave and fought their whole life and Achyuta wanted to work for the upliftment of such unsung heroes. These people were brilliant and knowledgeable, all they needed was the right guidance and a little bit of nurturing.

'Who could know these people and their battles better? Whenever, I see these young men and women struggling as we did, I want to help them.'

Achyuta eventually won the day. He managed to convince his mother. Nilimarani's fears were quenched by his arguments.

'Mother, please don't insist on my getting married. With your blessings, I will make this voyage with you by my side.'

Nilimarani reminisced how daring and enterprising her little Sukuta was as a child. He always had strong entrepreneurial abilities. He was capable of envisioning what boys and girls of his age couldn't. She began recollecting her own days at Jamshedpur. Nothing was given to her on a platter after her marriage. It was she who made it all work out by dint of sheer grit and hard work. Life itself was a big enterprise. She moved with the flow. Things kept falling into place. There were losses in the journey. There were difficult times when life seemed to have come to an end. There were lightning and thunder. Every situation in her life was a classroom and the myriad lessons she learnt, served her well.

She never interfered with her children's plans. Even when it came to her eldest son's marriage, she didn't impose her decision on him. When the proposal was brought by the girl's brother, she told them that the decision rested with Mantoo. When Mantoo visited the village a few days later, she asked him, 'So what have you decided about that girl? Her brother came to me for my approval.'

'Mother, I have no objection to the marriage proposal if you give your approval.'

The bride was from a poor family too and was the eldest child. They lost their parents and the girl shouldered the entire responsibility of the destitute family. Her story was similar to Mantoo's. Nilimarani's heart went out to her. She saw the girl only when she came home as a bride. She grew very fond of her daughter-in-law and they became more of friends. Nilimarani had become a kind of an atheist soon after the demise of her husband. She lost her faith in prayers and rituals. She even turned averse to religious rituals; she would brush them off as myths and misconceptions. She came to believe in one thing, that her duty towards her family was the only religion to follow. However, at the behest of her daughter-in-law, she tried to become a little religious. She was never overly critical. She knew that things were bound to change with the addition of daughters-in-law to the family because a marriage is not just the union of two individuals but rather an amalgamation of two families.

While blessing the newlyweds, she said, 'Understand the difference between ego and conscience. That's the most difficult thing to do in life. Many a time, people take ego to be their conscience and that becomes the reason for their downfall. Do what your conscience tells you, not what your ego prompts you to do. Never send a person back empty-handed if he has come to your doorstep with some hope. Before you become judgmental, put yourself in that person's shoes. Compromising on your values is a sign of weakness. Your end is as important as the means by which you achieve that end.'

Achyuta used to come to the village to check on his mother from time to time. However, she didn't ask him about his career, nor did she ask Mantoo to probe into the matter. She was confident that her children would do no wrong. Achyuta informed her that he had founded two modest institutions—Kalinga Institute of Industrial Technology (KIIT University) and Kalinga Institute of Social Sciences (KISS). While the former helped ambitious youngsters find jobs, the latter was for the upliftment of underprivileged tribal boys and girls.

'Rich people have no right to simply rest on their laurels and squander their money. They, too, have a responsibility towards society. What is the use of leaving behind a fortune for the future generation if you can't contribute to the welfare of others. One should live in the present. My institutions are faring well, Mother. They are involved in good work. I am happy seeing other people happy. I am happy that I am able to touch their lives and make a difference, no matter how small. I am very hopeful that the organizations will become well-known someday. They will show light to the people of the world.' With those words, Achyuta embraced his mother. She blessed him silently.

9

THE SPIRIT OF HUMANITY

No day is the same as the other; each dawn brings with it its own story. There was no exception to this maxim in Nilimarani's life.

Nilimarani woke up with daybreak, completely oblivious of what lay in store for her. She always tried her best to wear a smile, no matter what. She believed that there was light at the end of the tunnel. That day in particular put a song on her lips.

Whenever she was bored, she would come out to the front porch, spread a reed mat on the floor and lie down. The pristine beauty of the countryside was mesmerizing. Nature's beauty had a profound effect on her senses, opening the gateways from the outer world to the inner and it filled her heart with awe, wonder and appreciation of the Divinity.

How time flies! wondered Nilimarani. She was alone in the twilight of her life. Even today, she was resting on the front porch, watching the sun go down. A deep silence prevailed. There was nobody to disturb her. 'This silence is like a prayer,' mumbled Nilimarani, her face upturned to the sky. The deep-red ball of fire in the sky was perfect. She reminisced about those days when the house reverberated with the laughter and voices of her children. She wondered at how fast the years had passed by, how old she was getting; she was seventy-three now. She remembered the people and events that had shaped her life. She could faintly see the silhouettes of the familiar people before her. Every step of the way made a difference, for good or for worse.

Her daughters were married off and her sons were engaged in their professional pursuits. As they stayed in far-off towns and cities, they couldn't meet often. However, they visited their mother at times and she really looked forward to those visits. Suddenly, the laughter of children brought her back from her reverie. Her children had thrown her a surprise by visiting her that day along with the grandchildren. Although her children visited her sometimes, all of them coming together on that day, was something she didn't expect. She was overwhelmed with emotion. She felt her heart swelling with pride. It was an affirmation that she had achieved something in life. She rushed to the kitchen to check if she had everything she needed to prepare a hearty meal for the family. It was in her nature to first feed her children. Her eldest daughter-in-law quickly followed her into the kitchen. 'Don't worry, Mother. I will do the cooking. We have brought with us the ration. Please spend some time with the children,' she said warmly. Soon, her daughters, too, helped in the cooking.

Nilimarani was the oldest member in the house and the wisest as well, the matriarch. She knew that her children were living her legacy and were doing their best to hand down her wisdom to her grandchildren. She taught her children to love unconditionally and stay connected to their roots. And she felt happy when she noticed her grandchildren too following in her footsteps. In the infectious smile of her grandchildren, she saw a reflection of her husband's smile. Nilimarani taught her children and her grandchildren to bravely face the odds, after all some things are to be learnt the hard way.

'Happy birthday, Grandmother, happy birthday,' the children suddenly gathered around her and began singing the birthday song. They were joined in by their parents. Nilimarani was overjoyed. The happiness and joy of having the family together made her miss that important person in her life, the person who left her years ago. She had once mentioned to him how she insisted that her birthday be celebrated like that of the other boys in her neighbourhood when she a child. From that day, he was very particular about celebrating her birthday, but that tradition died down after his passing away. The thoughtfulness of her children and their warm gesture filled her heart. Celebrating a birthday at that age seemed a little awkward, but it was a pleasant surprise and she welcomed it. It was about having the family together and sharing the special day with them, and that was all that mattered to her.

The presence of the entire family led her down memory lane—those glorious escapes into the dark shades of the mango groves and the village forest during the afternoons, the fun and frolic she had had at the river bank, the time she spent in her beautiful garden and on the swing, with her many friends. Many of those groves had now vanished and the forest grew sparser with each passing year. Her family looked like a grove—there were the tall older trees, the middle-aged trees, the young trees and the saplings; each standing on its own, so independent and yet so bonded. The trees drew their nourishment from Mother Earth. With the seasons, the trees bore happy fruits and the thick foliage was covered with sparkling flowers, bringing a welcome relief. She was the 'head' tree in the grove under whose overarching presence the entire family thrived.

Nilimarani blushed as everyone broke into the birthday song and that endearing smile did not fade the whole day. She was so tied up in the responsibilities of raising her seven children all on her own that she had forgotten that there was a day, her birthday, that deserved to be celebrated.

'Please, children, let us steal your grandmother for a while? We have business to discuss. In the meanwhile, you all can go out and explore the village. Or you can just lie down in the front room and relax till lunch is served,' Achyuta addressed the children, who were playing with their grandmother. The children hugged their grandmother rapturously and romped out of the house into the garden. When they were gone, Nilimarani turned toward her sons, who squat cross-legged in front of her on the reed mat. 'I am glad you all came. Your village beckons you. The village is the essence of your being. You owe it to the village for what you are today. I wish you all to stay connected to your roots. This is where you belong. I don't expect you to settle here, but do keep visiting from time to time.'

Achyuta asked Nilimarani if there was anything she needed. He obviously meant to ask if he could build her a new house or purchase some cultivable land. The question hit her like a bolt out of the blue. She sat up. 'What is this all about, Sukuta?'

Sukuta hesitated for a second and then explained his idea to her. Yes, it was natural for her sons to want their mother to lead a comfortable life, especially because she had lived a life of drudgery for so long. She deserved to live a comfortable life after all that she has been through, but she never felt the need or demanded anything from her sons.

Her wants were beyond the mundane materialistic desires. She had a dream, a dream entirely her own; she had a longing to give back to the land which gave her so much and had enabled her to bring up her children. She felt an affinity towards the downtrodden and wanted to be involved in their betterment—there was something almost spiritual about it. She was at peace with herself. Nothing could break her in the past. Nothing would break her now. She had stood her ground, always, despite all tribulations. Whatever humble contribution she wanted to make towards her motherland, she would on her own. She wondered if Achyuta would join her in her mission of giving back to the motherland. *It will be worthwhile to take help from Achyuta, who is so accomplished in life and who, like me, wants to give back to society. One can benefit from his wisdom. I am sure he will not say no to me.* With her children's progress in life, she felt empowered and proud. She felt the ground where she stood was firmer.

Achyuta had once taken her to Bhubaneswar to show her the educational institutions that he had founded. Many years had come to pass since but the memory of that visit was still vivid. She only had a vague idea of what Achyuta was doing career-wise, but whatever little she had seen and known, was enough to impress her. He was moving steadily in his chosen mission; it was a new phase of existence for him now. He was never unhappy, despite the hardship and struggles he had to go through in life. He was truly delightful, well-judging and amiable.

After all, he had worked so hard to achieve that. With his charming and warm personality, he won people over wherever he went.

He had inherited his mother's sensibility and understanding of human nature. He was clear about what he wanted from life, and it was almost as if he had always prepared himself for that goal. He always reflected on the 'what' and the 'why' of poverty and realized that education was the key to emancipation from it and all its associated social evils. He already had many entrepreneurial ventures going in that direction. The institutions he founded proliferated and soon grew into a conglomerate of educational institutions with thousands of students studying various subjects. Nilimarani was particularly overwhelmed when she was taken to KISS, where about 10,000 tribal students were being given holistic education and free boarding. He founded this institute in 1992 along with KIIT as the philanthropic wing, with the sole aim of alleviating poverty through holistic education. The institute had rapidly grown, leveraged by KIIT, and had come to accommodate over 27,000 underprivileged tribal children who received free education from kindergarten to post-graduation, and life and vocational skills training along with free lodging, clothing and comprehensive healthcare. Almost 3,000 people were employed on the campus. She felt drawn towards the students there. She kept talking to them.

Suddenly, she came out of her reverie. Achyuta and Mantoo were still looking at her in anticipation. She was still silent. She looked at them both and gulped. Her eyes moistened.

The question posed by her sons had her thinking. On one side, there was hesitation, hesitation rising out of fear of rejection; she didn't know if Achyuta would agree to help her reach out to the underprivileged people in the village. On the other hand, she didn't doubt her children's commitment towards her; they had always stood by her and loved her. Her children, particularly, Achyuta was very attached to her and their village. Nilimarani always held firm, the belief, that charity begins at home and what better way to do that than work for the village that had provided the air to breathe, water to drink, food to eat and a roof to sleep under. She remembered how she used to once lumber up to the village forest to collect firewood and tubers, to the river bank for wild spinach to feed her children and the shallow waters for fish. In this village was the house she called her own. She remembered how she and Achyuta toiled in the fields, growing vegetables to be sold off in the market.

Nilimarani looked a little restless. *Are my children ashamed of this house?* She did get some renovation work done and had furnished it with some second-hand items included a cooking stove, a television, a refrigerator, a few chairs, a bed, a cupboard and all that she had managed to get from Mantoo. She did not do that for her own comfort. She only feared that her children and grandchildren would find it inconvenient without the basic comforts. As for her, she continued using the earthen stove and slept on the reed mat. She didn't have much use for the refrigerator too. She wondered if there was something she needed for a comfortable life but couldn't come up with anything.

Finally, putting her thoughts together, she said, 'The allowance you send me is good enough; in fact, more than enough. I don't want anything more for myself. You have been doing such good work already. I have everything I need. Since have you asked me, Sukuta, I want this village to be developed. This village has given us so much. Let there be happiness and peace in the village. No woman here should suffer the way I did. Let all be educated and trained so that they can earn two pence for a living. I will be happy if you focus on the development of the village.'

5 June 2006 was a memorable day in the history of Kalarabanka. The early morning sunshine filled the village with an air of exaltation. The warm glow of the sun brought everyone out of their homes. Every household in the village was filled with anticipation. It was after all the ushering of a new chapter in the history of the village—a chapter of prosperity, glory and honour. Every soul, young or old, in the village was bubbling with energy. Every passing bloke wore a wide smile on

his face and uttered a loud mirthful 'hello' on meeting fellow villagers. Over the past few years, the whole village had been working towards its upliftment and their efforts were finally paying off. The village was by now endowed with modern facilities and a strong infrastructure.

'Mother, have you heard the news?' Mantoo had asked as they sat in the front porch of her house, a month back. He was the president of the Nilimarani Charitable Trust now.

'No. What is it about?'

'Something the whole village will be delighted to know about. I thought I must tell you first. I met Achyuta in Bhubaneswar before coming here. He told me that the governor of the state, Rameshwar Thakur, will be visiting our village next month.'

'That's great news! It is indeed a milestone for our village.'

And from that day, for one whole month, the entire village had worked day and night in preparation for this big day. On 5 June 2006, the plaque was unveiled by the governor and Kalarabanka was declared as the first model village of the state.

In preparation for the day, young boys and girls had decorated the temporary gates at the entrance to the village. The streetlight posts were decorated. The houses too were decorated with colourful festoons and cut-outs. The village was swept clean. Colourful flags hung all along the roads. The newly constructed water-storage tank was already spruced up and decorated; it stood tall and looked majestic, as if standing as a testimony to the village's remarkable transition. The village was now easily accessible by a wide blacktopped all-weather road which connected it to the state highway. A bridge was constructed over the Taladanda canal that passed through the village.

The women of the village gathered at the newly set-up Village Women Self-help Group Centre and were busy organizing and putting up display stands. The employees at the post office were busy cleaning up their office and had come in their best attires. The doctor and his staff were tidying up the recently opened fifty-bedded dispensary. The bank manager was busy sorting out the paperwork and information on the banking record of the village. The constables at the police outpost were busy checking their uniforms and gears so as to look their best.

Some were beefing up the security arrangements in front of the temple in anticipation of a large gathering. Every tree trunk that lined the main road was given a fresh coat of white paint.

Nilimarani usually woke up late. Those days, she was attended to by a maid who stayed with her. Her maid was a young woman from the same village. She was destitute and needed shelter. She approached Nilimarani and asked if she could be of any service to her. Nilimarani needed a little help and could use some company. Thus, it was a win-win situation for both. In the village, house helps were treated as family. As a child, she was taught to treat maidservants with respect, love and compassion. And so, the girl was more of a friend to her.

As usual, her maid woke her up that day with a glass of water. Nilimarani finished her morning ablutions and had a breakfast of soaked flattened rice mixed with fresh curd and jaggery. She didn't like to have tea. She draped on a white saree, a white jacket and a pair of rubber slippers and stepped out of the house at about 10 a.m. She always took a round of the village. Like always, she went to all the institutions such as schools, dispensaries, library, post office and self-help group (SHG) that were started in the village. It was a routine she had been following for the last four years. It started with her supervising the construction of the temple complex. She would also take along with her, the village elders, to the temple complex. She greeted the workers at those institutes and asked them how things were progressing. Her visits to these institutions filled her with joy and satisfaction.

'Please come in, Ma,' a volunteer rushed out to welcome her as Nilimarani reached the office of the Nilimarani Charitable Trust.

Nilimarani was regarded as the iron-willed leader of the village. Women of all ages came to her for advice. Her aura of happiness and contentment wiped away the dejection of others and became a ray of hope for the needy. With her perseverance, all discord in her life was converted to harmony. People bowed before her. She was greatly instrumental in bringing about change in the village through her social work.

The volunteer fetched a chair and pleaded Nilimarani to take a seat. She smiled at the young woman. Soon, a host of young men and women gathered around her and a conference followed. After a while, a few of the village elders, who were members of the trust, also gathered there. The volunteers briefed her and the village elders about the upcoming events of the day. Mantoo, who had come to the village the previous evening to organize the event, was also present there. After a brief halt at the trust office, she perambulated to the Women Self-help Group Centre, where she met its members and conversed with them at length about their preparedness for the event. This organization helped the womenfolk of the village earn their livelihood using their skills. They were obliged to her. She was delighted to see them doing so well. Her eldest daughter-in-law was also there among the women as the guiding force.

On her way home, she walked down to the village dispensary too. She flipped through the register there at the behest of one of the staff. As she was going through the register for the in-patient ward, she noticed a woman in her late fifties walking up to her with hands folded. Her eyes were overflowing with tears. She recognized her at once and took her in her embrace. 'O Mother, we are able to get ourselves treated here in the village itself because of you and your worthy son, Achyuta.'

When she reached home, she rested on the recliner by the side of her bed. She called out to the maid, who was busy cooking in the kitchen, and asked, 'Achyuta will be here soon. Have you prepared food for him?' Her maid nodded in the affirmative.

She closed her eyes in a bid to catch a nap before going to the venue for the inaugural ceremony. Her spirits were elevated. She was glad that she had never called it quits even in the face of adversity. All good things in life start with a dream, with a desire and so did hers. Her husband, Anadi, too, had a dream, the dream to see his village prosper and become a developed one. Although Anadi used to be miles away from the village, in Jamshedpur, its welfare was always on his mind.

She always missed having her children around. Achyuta was an established educational entrepreneur and social worker and lived in

Bhubaneswar. Mantoo, too, lived in Bhubaneswar with his family. Her children wanted her to move to Bhubaneswar, but Nilimarani was not keen to move out of her village.

She remembered Achyuta's words when he had proposed to walk on the career path of social work: 'Mother, we have struggled through poverty and today we have reached a position where we can help others come out of poverty. I think God brought me here on this earth with a special purpose and I want to fulfill that purpose.'

Nilimarani never questioned what her children did. She had great confidence in them. 'Son, you have my blessings. You are so much like your father. But whatever you do, never forget your roots, this village.'

In 2004, Achyuta and Mantoo had visited the village to discuss the construction of a temple complex, which was her first wish. In the meeting, it was decided to have it built on the banks of the river Paika, which was no man's land. Community sentiment is the very essence of a village community and Nilimarani had an uncanny ability to sense the pulse of the village. Though the villagers were simple and sincere in their dealings with each other, they were critical of each other when it came to sharing of common facilities. They usually raised several questions if one attempted to undertake any development work in the village, but the proposal to build a temple was unanimously agreed upon. She had many plans for the village, but what better way to start the journey than by taking the Almighty's blessings?

Though she wasn't a religious person, unlike her husband, she appreciated the faith the villagers had in God. She loved visiting Puja pandals during Durga Puja celebrations though. So, her decision to construct the temple complex was suggestive of her compassion and understanding of the sentiments of the villagers.

Religion played a paramount role in the life of the villagers and religious rituals influenced every important agrarian and social activity in the village. On all such occasions, the villagers conducted religious ceremonies in the form of puja, mela or kirtan. The construction of a temple complex proved to be opportune and auspicious. It also brought together the villagers despite their differences.

The land on which the proposed temple was to be built had come to the village as a boon of Providence. Way back in the 1920s, a huge patch of land remained inundated with flood waters. When the government raised embankments along the river to restrict its flooding, this sixteen-acre patch of land became usable, but unfortunately it was not included in the government records. The villagers used this riverfront for grazing cattle, for cremation or for putting up brick kilns. Nilimarani's proposal, to build the temple complex, on that land was welcomed by the village elders, who themselves were not aware of the status of this land. The villagers resolved the issue of using the remaining land for the village's welfare within the community itself. In village communities, social control was informal and direct. The primary groups like the family and the neighbourhood acted as powerful agencies of social control. The traditional village panchayat performed a variety of tasks, including the maintenance of law and order, settling of disputes, the celebration of festivals and the construction of roads, bridges and water tanks.

The Nilimarani Charitable Trust, founded especially for the purpose of the development of the village, worked in perfect harmony with the panchayat. At the behest of Nilimarani, the elders took the panchayat into their confidence. Over the years, the culture of the village had become very static. Both Nilimarani and Achyuta had a vision to make it more dynamic and had laid great importance on cultural festivities. From the sociological point of view, villages are important because they preserve the culture of the country. The residents of Kalarabanka had great faith in the lofty ideals of Purusārtha and the doctrine of karma, and led a simple life. The temple project, therefore, received instant favour from the villagers of Kalarabanka as well as from the neighbouring villages. Help began flowing in from all quarters, for not just the construction of the temple but also other related developmental work. With the help of the villagers and the active support of Achyuta, the construction of the temple complex was completed in 2006 under the aegis of the Nilimarani Charitable Trust.

Due to poverty and the lack of adequate employment opportunities, the standard of living in the village was very low. Nilimarani was aware that most of the women in the village were uneducated and their social status was lower than that of their male counterparts. She herself had been a victim of that unfortunate situation. Factors such as child marriage, joint family system, traditional and age-old values and lack of education were further responsible for the poor plight of the women. She wanted to ease out the life of the village women. Luckily, Achyuta's foraying into the field of educational entrepreneurship was a blessing.

In 2002, with Achyuta's support, an English-medium school with classes from Kindergarten to Class X and residential accommodation was built in the village. The village primary school was upgraded to a high-school with boarding facility. The schools attracted children from the village and neighbouring villages too. Both the schools were made accessible to girl students. A community centre was set up with telephone communication. A medical dispensary, a library, a police outpost, a post office and a bank branch with locker and ATM facility were also established in the village. The pond was renovated and a water supply system was installed which brought water to each household. Trees were planted on the denuded land surfaces to reconstruct the environment.

Coming back to the governor's visit to Kalarabanka, he received a warm traditional welcome. He was taken around the village and shown all the recently opened facilities. He was indeed amazed to witness the transformation. Later, at a public meeting held in front of the temple complex, which was attended by thousands of people from Kalarabanka and the nearby villages, he appreciated the spirit of the Kalarabanka.

Nilimarani was seated in the audience with the other Trust members and fellow villagers. She was dressed in her usual attire—a white saree and a white jacket. She was pleased to witness new vigour, new enthusiasm and new zest among the villagers. The whole village was one big family. There was no jealousy, no hatred, just mutual cooperation and camaraderie. This was the best gift she could have given to the village.

The governor praised at length Nilimarani's sincerity and the sacrifices she had made for the development of the village. She was like a light in the darkness, always guiding the villagers. She painted a beautiful and colourful picture against the dark background of the village. 'I have immense respect for you, O' glorious Mother, who has given birth to the saviour of mankind, Sri Achyuta Samanta. You are indeed a very special leader, a legendary mother. You are one of a kind—unmatched, unparalleled. The transformation of this village, spearheaded by you and your son, is the stuff fairy tales are made of.'

The words of the governor rang in her ears and she could not control her tears. She was emotional, not for the praises that were showered on her, but because of the fact that she had been chosen by the Almighty to be the harbinger of change. She said a silent prayer, thanking Providence. Her tears were that of gratitude. She murmured a few words of blessings for her son Achyuta.

The governor's visit was widely covered by the media. Nilimarani was copiously praised as the uncelebrated matriarch of the village.

There was something in her persona that commanded respect. Life was a river of different situations for her—some favourable, some not so favourable, some not at all favourable. Each of those situations brought forth her real personality. Her travails became tales of glory and endurance, something for her fellow compatriots to draw inspiration from.

She always had leadership qualities, her friends looked up to her. Her father, who was respected by all, was a major influence in her life. She further learned that giving back to the community was an essential contribution. 'The process of transformation is a continuous process,' she often impressed upon the villagers.

Happy were the villagers to have such a woman, such a giving mother amidst them. She certainly deserved the respect and the admiration that came her way. Kalarabanka's transformation was crafted by two ordinary people with extraordinary grit and perseverance. Nilimarani and Achyuta gave back to their motherland in every sense of the term. A tiny spark of vision kindled by them lit up the present and the future of the whole village. The spark turned into a fire and the fire into a towering inferno.

The Nilimarani Charitable Trust was not one to rest on its laurels. It continued to work for the betterment of the village. Through it, all the villagers were covered with health insurance policies, so that they could have access to advanced medical care and treatment. Mobile phone towers were installed. Every household boasted of internet connectivity. The youth had access to computer education in the village itself. Solar-powered street lighting systems too were added. By 2016, the whole village was fully literate and its youth acquired higher degrees that helped them land well-paying jobs in nearby and far-off cities. The Trust contributed towards the development of its agrarian resources, too, through the organization, the Art of Giving. In 2014, the village was declared a 'Smart Village'.

Truly, Nilimarani was the hero of Kalarabanka.

10

THE JOURNEY, THE LEGACY...

Time and tide wait for none and neither does age. Every year lived takes away from one's life span, but adds to one's wisdom and experience. However, the final end spares none. Everyone who has taken birth has to die one day and everything will decay as time passes. Sooner or later, one will come to the threshold of life's end. Life has to come full circle. The manifest form will become the unmanifest again. That's the universal law.

With time, Nilimarani too strode towards old age. But unlike other people of her age, she wasn't very frail; she was energetic and affable. From the bassinet days when one had no care in the world, to the dancing and frolicking days of childhood, to the tingling teenage years, to the maturity of adulthood, and finally to the present, the journey had been a like roller-coaster for Nilimarani. Even during her old age, she loved the smell of the mud walls of her modest hut; the sights and sounds of the countryside still tickled her senses and brought a smile to her serene face.

Life had given her ample opportunities to validate the lessons she had learned from her parents, from her own experiences and from the scriptures she read. She was the shining star of the village, a shining star of love and compassion, a shining star that had a purpose—to light up the dark, to drive away human suffering, to revalidate the values of camaraderie, to reaffirm one's faith in humanity and be the brightest ray of hope for the villagers and all those who came in contact with her.

She was the greatest friend of the villagers and one of the greatest women to have ever walked the surface of the earth. Her serene presence and kind words comforted the wild waves of a storm-beaten heart; a touch of her hand was enough to soothe the restlessness of an aimlessly sprinting mind and her amiability made everyone feel at home. She was able to ignite the hearts and minds of the villagers.

1 August 2016. The day was a whirlwind of activities. Achyuta's day began quite early. He made a quick trip to Puri, the holy city of Lord Jagannath, situated some 60 kilometers from Bhubaneswar, where he mostly lived. He always paid a visit to Puri on the first day of every month. Having grown up in a remote village of Odisha, he was an ardent follower of Shree Jagannath. All cultural traditions and practices followed in the villages of Odisha were primarily connected with Lord Jagannath's temple. After returning to Bhubaneswar, he went straight to meet his mother, who was now in her late eighties. She stayed in Bhubaneswar too, those days, with her daughter Itina.

No sooner did he enter her room, she embraced him. She hugged him every time they met. He was her youngest son and therefore occupied a special corner in her heart. In her embrace, he not only felt his soul awaken but it also prepared him to reach out for more in his chosen career of social work. Her embrace rekindled the spark of resoluteness. They had a short but very invigorating conversation. They partook of the mahaprasad of Jagannath temple. 'Mahaprasad' is the term given to the fifty-six food items offered to Lord Jagannath in the holy Temple of Puri. He took her leave, promising to see her in the evening although he knew in his heart that he might not be able to take time out from his hectic schedule. I should spend more time with my mother, he thought to himself.

His schedule for the day was fixed. The itinerary included several meetings to be presided by him, besides sorting the piles of paperwork and the hundreds of correspondences that came in each day.

Things at work picked up speed as the day progressed. The last meeting of the day was over and Achyuta was about to call it a day. He quickly wrapped up his paperwork and kept them into the cotton bag he usually carried with him as he politely engaged in the casual post-meeting conversations with his colleagues. Finally, the attendant collected his bag and kept it in his car and Achuyta too headed for his car. Soon, he was on his way to his official quarter which was a twenty-minute drive from the office.

'Phew! It's been a great day. So far so good!' he said, taking a deep breath. He had been working hard and for long hours every day as the organization was expanding at a rapid pace. As the founder of the institute, he was striving to steer it in the right direction. There was no doubt that he had traversed a long way since his humble beginning to attaining global acclaim as an academician, educationist, social entrepreneur and a social activist, thanks to the unwavering faith and support of his mother. He dedicated his life to crusading against poverty, using education as the enabling tool. And he was fairly successful in achieving that. It filled him with pride to see his dream take shape and his institutions helping people in more ways than one.

Over the years, his perseverance, patience, farsightedness and diligent work brought him and the institutions he founded, much popularity and reputation globally. However, that kind of fame and recognition entailed added responsibilities and expectations. No wonder, he was always on his toes.

When he reached home, Kalu, his personal attendant, collected his handbag and the other files from the car.

It was monsoon season and the day was rather dull and gloomy. The weather forecasts showed incessant drizzle for the next twenty-four hours. However, luckily, the rain stopped briefly when he reached his quarter. Instinctively, he turned his head up to survey the sky. It was a new moon night. He decided to sit down in the front porch for a while before heading indoors. His quarter, IRC Village, wore a deserted look.

After spending a few moments on the porch, he went inside. He settled down in his favourite rocking chair in the drawing room. He placed his two cell phones, which he always carried with him, on the centre-table and started to shuffle through the newspapers and magazines neatly placed on it. He had already gone through them once in the morning and so now he simply scanned the headlines once again. Kalu got him a glass of cold water. What surprised him was the listlessness with which he was reading the paper. He was reading the same words over and over again without really understanding what he was reading. That was very unlike him.

He put the paper down and asked Kalu to switch on the television and put on his favourite channel, Kalinga TV, a channel founded by him. He began watching the 9 p.m. news. Staying updated with local, national and international news provided fodder for thought and helped him prepare for the upcoming day. Suddenly, a gust of wind started to blow. He looked at the sky through the window. 'Looks like it is going to rain heavily,' he whispered to himself.

Somewhere in the distance, a dog barked. Suddenly, one of his phones rang, startling him. He checked the display screen: Itina, it read.

'Hello, Itina. Good to hear from you.'

'Are you home already?'

'Why? Is everything fine?'

'Everything's fine. It's just that Mother was wondering if she could have a chat with you. Nothing serious, just like that...you must have had a hectic day, I guessed and I told her that. She insists on having a chat with you, you know how stubborn she can be at times.'

'Oh, yes, sure. I will have a word with her!'

Nilimarani was living with her youngest daughter, Itina for a couple of years now. She was younger to Achyuta by almost five years. She was an accomplished author and was also successfully heading Kadambini Media Pvt. Ltd, an organization founded by Achyuta for promoting art, culture and literature. She lived in a rented house close to the KIIT Group of Institutions (founded by him in 1992). The institute had grown into a huge educational conglomerate comprising the now globally famous KIIT University and several other institutes with a strength of over 30,000 students. To bring this institute to this level was no mean feat, especially when the group had over 10,000 employees, over 1,00,000 students and over a 1,000 people visiting the campus every day to attend various seminars, conferences and workshops. He also had the responsibility of managing KISS, which was again a mammoth task in itself.

Despite his hectic schedule, not a day went by without Achyuta paying a visit to his mother whenever he was in Bhubaneshwar. However, due to time constraint, his meetings with his mother grew painfully brief and he felt sad about it. She always had a lot of concerns about his health. Her hands still bore signs of hardship. They had cradled seven infants, fed them; they had dug up tons of earth to raise a small kitchen garden, planted numerous vegetables, brought tons of water on her head to water the plants and helped them grow, bear flowers and fruits. She had fallen countless times too. Her slender fingers and her palms still bore the tell-tale signs of a life lived through struggle and hardship. However, the same rough and creased hands comforted him.

Every struggle in her life shaped her into the person that she was. Even at that advanced age, she was absolutely alert. Her face radiated contentment. She went about sincerely fulfilling her responsibility as a mother, without expecting anything in return. Although she was loved and admired by one and all in the village and was a force to reckon with, she never let success go to her head. She was humble and down-to-earth. Her life was governed by a great sense of reasonableness and unshakable integrity.

Achyuta considered himself very fortunate to have a person like her in his life. They were each other's friend, confidante, partner and companion through thick and thin. They were soulmates, so to say.

'Hello.' The voice of Nilimarani at the other end of the phone nudged him out of his thoughts.

'Sukuta, why didn't you come for lunch today?' she asked and quickly added, 'I missed you.'

'I am so sorry, Mother. It was a very busy day for me. After returning from Puri I haven't had a minute's rest. I had to catch up with a number of officials.'

'I know. You have always been a workaholic. Did you have your lunch, Sukuta?'

He had just had some light snacks and watermelon juice for lunch and some more snacks in the evening. However, if he told her that she would be upset. 'Yes, Mother, I had some mahaprasad in the Jagannath temple.'

'Have you eaten your dinner?'

'No, not yet, Mother!'

Nilimarani was a cheerleader for Achyuta, sometimes in visible ways, sometimes in subtle or unspoken ways. She always encouraged him in his work. Her children had gone hungry for days during their childhood and that was something she could never forgot. Even after her children had grown up and were successful in their own right, she would insist on them eating in front of her. Whenever guests came to the house, she would not leave them without feeding them a proper meal. She would always enquire if her children had eaten. She was particularly concerned about her youngest son, Achyuta, because he was a bachelor.

'Have your dinner and go to bed early. You must not starve. It will hurt me if you starved despite having everything. I know you must have had a long day as usual. Take care of yourself!'

There is no love so strong, so everlasting, so selfless, so pure and so devoted like a mother's. Her words felt like a warm embrace and made him feel safe and secure.

'Mother, I love you,' he mumbled under his breath. He wished he had the courage to say that out loud, but they were not groomed to be so expressive in the villages.

'Yes, Mother, I will! You should sleep now. Take care. Good night!'

Nilimarani passed the phone to Itina and they chatted for a while. Itina informed that Mantoo was there with Nilimarani all through the evening and both had a great time gossiping. He had recently retired from service and he too lived in Bhubaneswar with his family. His wife, who was still in service, and he visited Nilimarani every evening without fail. Being the eldest son, he occupied a special place in her heart.

However, that evening, Mantoo had come alone, as his wife was held up in office.

They talked for nearly two and a half hours. After Mantoo left, she went inside the prayer room to listen to the spiritual scriptures and chants read by her personal maid. This was her routine. She had mentioned to him how sometime she felt a bit tired. Nothing to be worried, it is just a natural part of ageing, she had insisted. She was checked by her brother, who was a doctor himself, at weekly intervals.

Achyuta, too, was a stickler for discipline. After his phone call with his mother and sister, he took a relaxing warm shower, had a light dinner and hit the bed exactly at 10 p.m. Since it was raining intermittently, he decided against taking his customary post-dinner walk. And after all, working for almost eighteen hours every day does take its toll on one's body and mind. So, he did some light exercises instead before going to bed to relax his muscles and de-stress. He believed that most of the stress stemmed from unresolved issues or work left to be completed. He did not like to carry the stress of one day to the next, so he always took a walk at night or did some stretching in the house itself.

Kalu came into his room, placed a jug of water and a glass on the bedside nightstand, drew all the curtains, switched on the night lamp and switched off the main lights before retreating, softly closing the door behind Achyuta. Ravi Biswal, the steward at the quarter, had already left for the day.

Silence prevailed in the room but for the sound of the rain. Despite physical exhaustion, for some reason Achyuta could not fall asleep; a rumble in his stomach made him toss and turn for hours. At some point, he got so bored of his sleeplessness that he got up from his bed, walked to the window and stared out at no particular object. *Why this restlessness? I always fall asleep on time.* He went back to bed. Fatigue was getting the better of him, but his sleep was disturbed. He sat up in his bed, poured himself a glass of water and gulped it down. He wished to be a kid again so that he could cuddle by his mother's side and fall into a blissful slumber. An uncanny pang of separation from his mother tormented him, pushing his sleep further away. It was almost dawn.

The sound of the rain grew louder as it lashed against the window panes and the roof, the whining of the wind was fiercely loud too. He kept tossing and turning in bed, unable to get any sleep. The intermittent chorus of the street dogs barking and howling punctuated by the thunderclaps every now and then prevented sleep from descending upon Achyuta. The ominous howling of the dogs sent chills down his spine. 'Get some sleep,' he kept telling himself, but in vain. He drifted into a sleep but woke up soon after, a peculiar restlessness gripping his senses. He felt his mouth become dry and he had another glass of water. Then, he sat on the edge of the bed, covered his face with his hands and focused on his breathing to relax. When his breathing steadied, he lay down in bed. Even before he knew it, he had fallen asleep.

Knock, knock, knock...

'Is anyone home?' The voice was faint but sounded familiar. 'Open the door!' A shrill female voice called out again.

The raps on the door grew louder and louder. Suddenly, the door flung open with a loud thud and a chilly wind gushed into the room. He froze. A light flashed in his direction. There stood a blurry figure. He struggled to get up, but his body was too stiff to move. *Is that a woman? Who could she be? What is she doing here, at this time?*

'Who's there?' he wanted to yell, but his lips were tightly pursed. He couldn't force them open.

Suddenly, a dove flew into the room out of nowhere and then flew out again. Achyuta woke up. He looked around the room, bewildered. He switched on the main lights. His heart was still pounding in this chest. *Was that a dream?* He strained his ears to check if there indeed was someone at the door or was it all his imagination. He called out.

There was no reply. Sleepily, he walked up to the window. It was still pouring hard and the wind was howling. He shot a quick glance at the wall clock. *Still two more hours till dawn.* He had never felt like this before. He went back to bed, but didn't switch off the main lights.

Knock, knock...

Achyuta was woken up by a light tap on the front door. He walked to the window and drew the curtains. It was almost 4.00 a.m. The rain had stopped by then. There was another knock on the door.

'Kalu? Is that you?' He called out, looking at the wall clock.

'Yes, sir, it's me. There is a very urgent message for you, sir!' He sounded frantic and shaky.

What could it be? He opened the door and asked Kalu to come in. He was accompanied by Ravi. They were hesitant, their eyes moist.

'What is it, Kalu? Ravi, is everything okay?'

Their lips were trembling.

'What is it?' he asked again, worried.

Kalu's and Ravi's heads hung low as the latter finally spoke, his voice subdued, 'Iti ma'am asked me to break the news to you carefully, so as not to shock you.' He drew a deep breath and continued, 'She called a while ago and sounded very disturbed. You must rush to her quarter, sir. Something's not right with Mother. I have already sent for the driver.'

Achyuta froze; his legs and hands were numb and weightless. He was shattered. *Is this a dream? No, this is real.* He looked at the wall clock. It was thirty minutes past four.

Nilimarani's smiling face flashed in his mind again and again. He didn't realize, but tears were trickling down his cheeks.

There was nothing to suggest that Nilimarani had been suffering or was unwell. Who would have known that it was going to be a memorable day in her children's life, memorable not because of any extraordinary accomplishment but for being the saddest day of their lives. Death was sudden. She was no more. The hero of Kalarabanka was no more. Nilimarani breathed her last in the warm embrace of her daughter Itina that morning.

On that fateful day, Itina had retired to her room after dinner. She had had a hectic day and was tired. She had fallen asleep no sooner than she hit her bed. At about 3 a.m., there was an s.o.s call from Sulochana, Nilimarani's housemaid who slept by her bedside. Itina woke up with a jerk and rushed downstairs to her mother's room. Sulochana was holding her by her shoulders as she struggled to breathe; her chest was heaving. Itina rushed to her. She asked Sulochana to rub Nilimarani's hands while she called Dr R.N. Samanta, Nilimarani's youngest and only brother.

'Hello, uncle, mother is not well and...er...it looks serious...' she narrated Nilimarani's condition in a single breath.

'I am coming right away...' replied Nilimarani's brother and hung up.

Nilimarani's condition deteriorated through the night. She kept on moaning and mumbling, 'Itina, I'm not going to make it this time. Ask your siblings to come...'

Itina consoled her, 'Mother, nothing will happen to you. Uncle will be here any minute. I have already informed him and he is on his way; you will be alright.'

Nilimarani had immense faith in her youngest brother as a doctor. She never treated him as her brother; he was more like a son. He was born the year she got married and she took care of him when their mother passed away.

Although Nilimarani had heart issues, she was never hospitalized. Now, suddenly, she started to gasp and her chest began to heave. Itina was at her wit's end. She began rubbing her shoulders, chest and back. Dr Samanta soon arrived. An ambulance from KIMS Hospital was called too.

Achyuta sped towards Iti's official residence, fraught with worry. His mother's serene face, her endearing smile and her whole life flashed in his mind's eye. He didn't have very vivid memories of his father as he had passed away when he was very young; his mother was everything to him. She was his friend, philosopher and guide. Like any other mother, she, too, took pride in his accomplishments, always encouraging and cheering for him to do better, be better. With every memory of her, tears trickled down his cheeks. He longed for his mother's warm embrace and prayed for her well-being

When he reached Itina's residence, the security guard rushed to tell him that Nilimarani had been taken to the hospital and that everybody was there. Without wasting a second, he headed to the hospital. *Is it that serious?* A strange sense of fatigue crept up his body and his mind went numb.

It didn't take him long to reach the hospital. Itina, Mantoo and a few other relatives were standing outside the ward, sobbing. A strange sense of loss gripped him. He went inside the room and lumbered to the foot of the bed. Nilimarani's eyes were closed, but her face beamed with the resoluteness that she had been so well known for all her life. He stood by the bed and kept looking at her face. He felt two hands caressing his shoulders. 'I'm sorry, Samanta sir, we couldn't save her. She had breathed her last when she was brought in,' said the doctor. His uncle, Dr Samanta, who was there beside the doctor, nodded to confirm.

'Achyuta, she has left us for her heavenly abode. We will not get to talk to her and listen to her again. She is gone for good. Achyuta, she is gone to the other world, the world of spirits.' Mantoo held on to his mother's toes and bent down to bid her farewell.

'Mother, may your soul rest in peace.' Itina was inconsolable. Her mother's death ripped her. Her mother, her best friend, her 'everything' was gone, snatched from her.

Ever since Nilimarani shifted to Bhubaneswar to live with Iti, the mother–daughter relationship blossomed. Iti, who almost played the role of a mother to Nilimarani, knew everything about her: her habits—no matter how insignificant, preferences and idiosyncrasies.

Nilimarani would often say, 'Maybe in some life, you *were* my mother.' As a mother, Nilimarani, too, knew her children well. She gave her children ample chances to see the beauty of the world in which they lived despite the ugly face of poverty that was their constant companion in their growing years. As a child, she considered her mother to be a goddess. At times loving and forgiving, and at times, stern and unrelenting.

Iti was almost like her mother's extension. She was Nilimarani's heart and soul, and in her own words 'the best thing that could have happened to her, the cause of many laughs and a few tears too.'

With Nilimarani gone, the children felt deprived of parental love, care and affection. They had already lost their father and now their mother too was no more. It was too harsh a blow for anyone to endure.

The news of Nilimarani's demise spread like wildfire and people started pouring in to pay their last respects. Her body was placed in the front porch so that the well-wishers could pay their homage. The beautiful fragrance of incense sticks and fresh flowers sanctified the environment. She looked so much at peace—as though she was sleeping peacefully.

Nilimarani attended many socio-cultural functions organized by the Kadambini Media Limited, an organization founded by Achyuta and run by Iti, and hence was known to many people. She herself was nothing short of a celebrity because of the transformational work she initiated in Kalarabanka. Among the mourners were statesmen, social workers, representatives of the media, writers, publishers, littérateurs, members of the KIIT and KISS fraternity, neighbours, people from Kalarabanka and other neighbouring villages. They were all overwhelmed with grief and consoled each other. They shared thoughts and condolences with our family. Goodbyes and tears morphed into memories that were so close to their hearts.

As a mother, Nilimarani taught her children to be strong because she knew they'd have to face life on their own. It was a tough time for her children, but they remembered their mother's words every time they felt like they were falling apart. She gave them much more than a place to call home, she gave them a place in her heart. They had always known Nilimarani as an inspirational woman, a loving mother and a great human being. As a mother, she fought battles which she was on the verge of losing. Even when she was fighting lost battles, she never felt defeated. She was mother not only to her children, but to every soul she touched. The people remembered the beautiful moments spent in her company and the love, compassion and blessings she showered on them and their families. Life would go on, but there would always be a special place in their hearts, reserved for this woman, their Mother, who sacrificed her comforts for the larger good. She was the matriarch, the uncrowned queen and the unsung hero of Kalarabanka. That was the legacy Nilimarani left behind. She was like a mother and friend to the whole village. She entered the public field at an age when people normally rest in their cozy homes. She showed exemplary leadership. Every institution in the village bore the footprints of her great vision and compassion.

For her children, Nilimarani was more than just a mother. She was the centre of their universe and their very heartbeat. Losing someone so special in their life was unthinkable. Losing her was like losing the only person in the world who always understood them without them saying it in that many words. Her life is exemplary.

For Achyuta, nothing could come close to a hug from his mother. Now, he missed her warm and affectionate embrace. A mother's love is unconditional and forever. She nurtured him from deep within her soul.

Even after her death, her legacy lives on through the many verses, idioms and sayings which she often quoted to her children and her grandchildren. These nuggets of wisdom are priceless, as they are rooted in real-life experiences and no classroom teaching or books can compare. She lived a simple life but gave her children a truly good upbringing, making sure they excelled in their own calling. That is worth an applause, especially when young people going astray in the face of poverty is not uncommon.

Hearing from people who have benefitted from the developmental activities undertaken by her at the village level is truly gratifying. She filled them with hope. What she learned at the workshop called life continued to help her stay strong, despite the untimely demise of her husband. Looking back, her struggles were both heartbreaking and inspiring. Providence's designs are mysterious.

People live and die, but some leave behind legacies. Mothers never die. They continue to live in the legacy they leave behind. Nilimarani has left behind not only memories for her children but also a legacy as a legendary mother and a social worker. She lived a very modest life, detached from any worldly desires even though she was born into a very opulent family. Her upbringing made her humble and grounded. She took courageous decisions in her life. She valued truth and propriety over everything else. She never gave in to vanity and accepted the reality as it was. She was empathetic. Her dreams were not frivolous but down to earth. She giggled amongst the flowers in her childhood days, but didn't mind embracing the thorns. She never let her anguish show on her face. She was strong-minded and always stood her ground like a rock and her steps never faltered.

As was her last wish, her body was taken to Kalarabanka. The casket carrying her body was placed in their ancestral house for the villagers to pay their final respects. The sight was overwhelming as thousands poured in to offer their prayers and homage. People from Kalarabanka and other nearby villages queued up to have the last glimpse of their beloved Mother, the Matriarch of Kalarabanka, their queen, their hero.

Men, women and children from far and near thronged Kalarabanka to attend her funeral. The poor and underprivileged were the most sincere mourners; theirs was the life she had touched the most. There were mothers who once were dejected in life, but Nilimarani gave them hope and a reason to live. They beat their chests and cursed their luck for losing a mother.

After the procession around the village, her body was taken to the funeral ground, where many had gathered. A soft breeze of pain and agony blew. The lightning in the sky crackled and the clouds splintered as hushed voices gave way to loud chanting, 'Hail Nilimarani Samanta! Hail O' Mother! Hail the hero of Kalarabanka! You will be in our hearts till eternity. Hail the holy soil of Kalarabanka that cradled you.'

The funeral ground reverberated with the sobbing of people as the funeral pyre was lit and the smoke rose up to mingle with the clouds. Her ethereal soul rose along with the smoke to take its place in heaven. She was perhaps, at a vantage point, thinking, I am finally home. The people of Kalarabanka lost their hero, but she still continues to dwell in their hearts.